Sudoku Techni

Welcome to Related Values Chaining

Cliff McQuesten

Previously published as *Sudoku Chaining* by Cliff McQuesten

Table of Contents

Puzzle Description

A Sudoku puzzle has 9 **rows**, identified as "A" through "I", and 9 **columns**, numbered 1 through 9. There are 81 **cells** which are grouped into 9 **boxes**, numbered 1 through 9. Each cell may contain a number from one to nine, and each number can only occur once in each row, column and box.

Each box has 3 **row segments** and 3 **column segments** as illustrated below.

It is helpful to use the term **line** to indicate either a row or a column, and **unit** to indicate a row, column, or box. Each unit has 9 cells. A **candidate value** refers to a possible value for an unknown puzzle cell. A sample puzzle is shown below.

A Mega Sudoku puzzle has 16 rows, 16 columns, 256 cells and 16 boxes. These puzzles can be very challenging.

Wikipedia has entries for *Sudoku*, *Glossary of Sudoku* and more.

A difficult puzzle

	Col 1	Col 2	Col 3	Col 4	Col 5	Col 6	Col 7	Col 8	Col 9
Row A	.	.	.	8	.	.	.	2	.
Row B	.	.	.	.	3	.	.	.	7
Row C	.	.	.	.	9	1	3	.	.
Row D	6	.	8	2	.	.	.	.	.
Row E	.	4	.	.	.	.	.	6	.
Row F	.	.	1	.	.	.	.	.	5
Row G	4	6	.	.	.	.	.	.	.
Row H	.	.	7	.	.	.	.	.	9
Row I	.	8	9	.	1	7	.	.	.

The value for the cell "row A, column 1" is unknown and is shown as ".".; the value for cell "A-4" is **8**.

The first box contains cells A-1, A-2, A-3, B-1, B-2, B-3, C-1, C-2 and C-3.

"." indicates an unsolved (unknown) cell.

The first *row segment* for box 3 (which is for Row A) is highlighted. And the first *column segment* for box 4 (which is for Column 1) is highlighted.

5

Solution to Puzzle

	Col 1	Col 2	Col 3	Col 4	Col 5	Col 6	Col 7	Col 8	Col 9
Row A	9	3	4	8	7	6	5	2	1
Row B	8	1	6	5	3	2	4	9	7
Row C	7	5	2	4	9	1	3	8	6
Row D	6	7	8	2	5	4	9	1	3
Row E	3	4	5	1	8	9	7	6	2
Row F	2	9	1	7	6	3	8	4	5
Row G	4	6	3	9	2	5	1	7	8
Row H	1	2	7	3	4	8	6	5	9
Row I	5	8	9	6	1	7	2	3	4

Overview of Techniques

The basic techniques *One Segment for Rows*, *One Segment for Columns*, *One Block for Rows* and *One Block for Columns* are straightforward. These techniques don't use chaining. They are included to provide a basis for the *Two Segments* techniques, which are more complicated. They are described in the Section "Background Techniques".

xy-chaining is also a basic technique. An xy-chain is a series of *related* two-valued cells that can be linked together. *"related"* means that two linked cells have a common candidate value and share the same row, same column and/or same box. Basic xy-chaining, unenhanced, is described in the Section *xy-chaining*. xy-chaining can be enhanced to use Related Values and Tree Chaining.

Related Values Chaining, Tree Chaining and the Chaining Methods are based on xy-chaining.

Related Values Chaining extends xy-chaining to analyze row-, column- and box-interactions between chain links and cells that are not part of the chain. A group of two or more chains are considered, depending on the Chaining Method used. Related values analysis can:

- solve puzzle cells that are not links in the chain
- determine additional cells that can be used as chain links, leading to longer chains

Tree Chaining extends xy-chaining for multiple branches and incorporates Related Values Chaining. A "Chain Tree" is a multi-branched chain.

Each Chaining Method is a front end to chaining utilizing special treatment for the first one or two cells in the chain, allowing a three-, four- or five- valued cell for the chain head, or two 3-valued cells for the chain head and the second cell. The Chaining Methods are used with Related Values Chaining and Tree Chaining. The Methods are:

- Three values Chaining
- Four values Chaining
- Five values Chaining
- Dual Triple Chaining

Enhanced xy-chaining can be considered as a Chaining Method that doesn't use special treatment for the first one or two cells in the chain.

The *Corners Technique* is complicated. It considers a single candidate value and looks for a pattern across multiple cells in four boxes that form the corners of a rectangle. If the pattern is matched the candidate value can be removed from one corner cell.

The *"Junior Exocet" (JExocet) Technique* is for 9 x 9 Sudoku puzzles only. This technique is **very** complicated. It uses a pattern involving:

- Two Base Cells
- Two Target Cells

- a Companion Cell for the first Target
- a Companion Cell for the second Target
- a Mirror Node consisting of two *near by(*)* cells for the first Target
- a Mirror Node consisting of two *near by(*)* cells for the second Target
- Three sets of six "S Cells" that are outside of the base- and targets- boxes, as shown in the Section *Exocet Technique*.

There are two main patterns for JExocets, the first uses a three digit pattern and the second uses a four digit pattern. Further, the pattern may be either row based or column based. And the pattern may be either *diagonal* or *aligned*.

(*) The *near by* cells are in the same box and in the same row for a row-based pattern, or the same column for a column-based pattern.

The *BigFish Techniques* are straightforward, however BigFish-4 is more involved than BigFish-2. These techniques consider a single candidate value and look for a pattern across sets of four, nine or sixteen cells. If the pattern is matched the candidate value can be removed from certain related cells.

The *Two Segments* Techniques are straightforward, however they are for 16 x 16 Sudoku puzzles only. They consider a single candidate value and look for a pattern involving four, aligned, boxes. If the pattern is matched the candidate value can be removed from certain related cells.

The *Corners, JExocet, BigFish and Two Segments* Techniques don't use chaining. They are described in Sections below, *Corners Technique, Exocet Technique, BigFish Techniques, Appendix A* and *Two Segments Techniques, Appendix B*.

Applicability and webpage

Most of the techniques are applicable equally to traditional 9 x 9 Sudoku puzzles and Mega Sudoku 16 x 16 puzzles; however:

- the JExocet Technique is for 9 x 9 puzzles only
- the Two Segments Techniques are for 16 x 16 puzzles only

The strategies range from simple to complex. Some are only necessary for diabolical (difficult) Sudoku puzzles. A few are not practical for manual (paper and pencil) use – for these computer processing is envisioned.

These techniques are relatively simple :

- the One Segment and One Block techniques
- xy-chaining
- the BigFish techniques, especially BigFish-2
- the Two Segments techniques; note that they are for 16 x 16 puzzles only

Related Values Chaining, Tree Chaining and the Chaining Methods are difficult to use.

The Corners Technique is complicated.

The Junior Exocet Technique is very complicated.

There is a webpage for this book at SudokuChaining.YahooSites.com.

Background Techniques

Four techniques are described which form a basis for the advanced technique *Two Segments* :

- One Segment for Rows
- One Segment for Columns
- One Block for Rows
- One Block for Columns

These techniques are applicable to both 9 x 9 and 16 x 16 Sudoku puzzles. They look for a pattern for a single candidate value; chaining is not involved.

One Segment for Rows

This technique is performed for rows, it considers a single candidate value.

- For a 9 x 9 puzzle, the technique looks for a pattern across a horizontal group of three boxes for the same rows, e.g. boxes 1 - 3 for rows A, B and C (may be termed rows 1, 2 and 3).
- For a 16 x 16 puzzle, the technique looks for a pattern across a horizontal group of four boxes for the same rows, e.g. boxes 1 - 4 for rows A, B, C and D (may be termed rows 1 - 4).

To determine a pattern match look for a box that has the candidate value in only one row segment. Each of the three or four boxes is considered, one at a time. If the pattern is matched the value can be removed from the corresponding row segment for the other boxes in the group.

Example for a 9 x 9 puzzle: the candidate value 1 is in box 1 only in row A. So 1 can be purged for the row segments for row A in boxes 2 and 3. See the example puzzle subset below - **cell A-5 in box 2 can be changed** from { 1, 2, 3, 5, 6 } to { 2, 3, 5, 6 }; and **cell A-7 in box 3 can be changed** from { 1, 2, 5 } to { 2, 5 }.

And consider the candidate value 3 - in box 1 it appears only in row A. So 3 can be purged for the row segments for row A in boxes 2 and 3 - **cell A-5 in box 2 can be changed** from { 2, 3, 5, 6 } to { 2, 5, 6 }.

One Segment for Rows example puzzle subset

The row segment that forms the pattern is shown highlighted. The value of interest is 1, the box of interest is box 1, and the row of interest is row A.

There is another pattern match for the value 3, for box 1, for row A.

	Col 1	Col 2	Col 3	Col 4	Col 5	Col 6	Col 7	Col 8	Col 9
Row A	1 3	3 5 9	1 3 9	5 6	1 2 3 5 6	8	1 2 5	4	7
Row B	4 7 8	4 5 7	4 5	9	1 2 3 5 7	1 2 3 7	1 2 8	6	1 2 3 8
Row C	2	6	7 8	4	1 3 5 7	1 3 7	1 5 8 9	3 8 9	1 3 8 9

One Segment for Columns

This technique is performed for columns, it considers a single candidate value.

- For a 9 x 9 puzzle, the technique looks for a pattern across a vertical group of three boxes for the same columns, e.g. boxes 1, 4 and 7 for columns 1, 2 and 3.
- For a 16 x 16 puzzle, the technique looks for a pattern across a vertical group of four boxes for the same columns, e.g. boxes 1, 5, 9 and 13 for columns 1, 2, 3 and 4.

To determine a pattern match look for a box that has the candidate value in only one column segment. Each of the three or four boxes is considered one at a time. If the pattern is matched the value can be removed from the corresponding column segment for the other boxes in the group.

One Block for Rows

This technique is performed for rows, it considers a single candidate value.

- For a 9 x 9 puzzle, the technique looks for a pattern across a horizontal group of three boxes for the same rows, e.g. boxes 1 - 3 for rows A, B and C.
- For a 16 x 16 puzzle, the technique looks for a pattern across a horizontal group of four boxes for the same rows, e.g. boxes 1 - 4 for rows A, B, C and D.

To determine a pattern match look for a row that has the candidate value in only one of the group of three or four boxes. If the pattern is matched the value can be removed for the other row segments for the box.

Example for a 9 x 9 puzzle: the candidate value 9 is in Row B only in box 1. So 9 can be purged for the other row segments in box 1. See the example puzzle subset below:

- **cell A-1 in box 1 can be changed** from { 2, 3, 4, 5, 7, 9 } to { 2, 3, 4, 5, 7 }
- **cell A-2 can be changed** from { 1, 2, 3, 4, 9 } to { 1, 2, 3, 4 }
- **cell A-3 can be changed** from { 1, 2, 3, 7, 9 } to { 1, 2, 3, 7 }.

One Block for Rows example puzzle subset

The row segment that forms the pattern is shown highlighted. The value of interest is 9, the box of interest is box 1, and the row of interest is row B.

	Col 1	Col 2	Col 3	Col 4	Col 5	Col 6	Col 7	Col 8	Col 9
A	2 3 4 5 7 9	1 2 3 4 9	1 2 3 7 9	1 3 5 8 9	1 2 4 5 8 9	1 2 3 5 9	6	1 2 3	1 2 3 4
B	2 3 4 9	8	1 2 3 9	1 3 6	1 2 4 6	2 3	1 2 3 4	5	7
C	2 3 5	1 2 3 4	6	1 3 5	1 2 4 5	7	1 2 3 4	8	9

One Block for Columns

This technique is performed for columns, it considers a single candidate value.

- For a 9 x 9 puzzle, the technique looks for a pattern across a vertical group of three boxes for the same columns, e.g. boxes 1, 4 and 7 for columns 1, 2 and 3.
- For a 16 x 16 puzzle, the technique looks for a pattern across a vertical group of four boxes for the same columns, e.g. boxes 1, 5, 9 and 13 for columns 1, 2, 3 and 4.

To determine a pattern match look for a column that has the candidate value in only one of the group of three or four boxes. If the pattern is matched the value can be removed for the other column segments for the box.

xy-chaining

An xy-chain is a series of *related* two-valued cells that can be linked together. *"related"* means that two linked cells have a common candidate value and share the same row, same column and/or same box. The two linked cells may or may not be identical.

The first cell in a chain is called the *chain head* cell.

For a *chain head* cell two chains can be analyzed, one for the chain head's smaller candidate value and the other for the chain head's larger candidate value. For the first chain, the smaller candidate value is termed the *head-link* value and the larger candidate value is termed the *head-other* value. For the second chain, the larger candidate value is the *head-link* value and the smaller candidate value is the *head-other* value. Initially the *head-link* value is assumed to be the cell's value (is used as the *chaining value* for the cell), and is used as the current linking value.

"Chaining progression" means to look for a *related* two-valued cell that has the current linking value as a candidate. Then that cell's other candidate value becomes the "next linking value" and is used as the *chaining value* for the cell. This cell's location is termed "current-row", "current-column". An example puzzle for xy-chaining is shown below.

For the third and subsequent cells in the chain, the "next linking value" is compared to the *head-other* value - if equal purging the *head-other* value may be possible:

1. Type A Purge If the current cell is in the same box as the chain head cell then the *head-other* value can be purged from any other cells in the box, excluding the chain head, that have the *head-other* value as a candidate.
2. Type B Purge If the current cell is in the same row as the chain head cell then the *head-other* value can be purged from any other cells in the row, excluding the chain head, that have the *head-other* value as a candidate.
3. Type C Purge If the current cell is in the same column as the chain head cell then the *head-other* value can be purged from any other cells in the column, excluding the chain head, that have the *head-other* value as a candidate.
4. Type D Purge If the cell in the "current column" and the same row as the chain head has multiple candidate values that include the *head-other* value then the *head-other* value can be purged from the cell. This is shown in the Example below.
5. Type E Purge If the cell in the "current-row" and the same column as the chain head has multiple candidate values that include the *head-other* value then the *head-other* value can be purged from the cell. This is shown in the second example below.

A Type F *chaining conflict* has occurred if during chaining progression a link could be formed back to the chain head and the current linking value is equal to the *head-link*. If so a Purge can be performed:

6. Type F Purge the *head-link* value can be purged from the chain head cell.

Chaining progression ends when, for the current chain cell, a link to another cell cannot be found.

A check for a Type G chaining conflict can be performed when a chain link is added, or only upon end of chain. For this analysis the original values of the chain cells is not used –

the cell's *chaining value* is used. A Type G *chaining conflict* has occurred if:

- a chain cell has a *chaining value* that is in it's row-, column- or box- more than one time as a *chaining value*
- a chain cell's row-, column- or box- has no candidate for the value 1
- a chain cell's row-, column- or box- has no candidate for the value 2
- ...
- a chain cell's row-, column- or box- has no candidate for the value 9

If a Type G chaining conflict occurs then a purge can be performed:

    7. Type G Purge the *head-link* value can be purged from the chain head cell.

After performing a Type A - G Purge, chaining progression ends.

Example 1 for xy-chaining

For this example, the chain head is cell E-8. The first pass uses the value 5 for the *head-link* value. The second pass uses 8 for the *head-link*. The second pass is described for this example.

	Col 1	Col 2	Col 3	Col 4	Col 5	Col 6	Col 7	Col 8	Col 9
Row A	9	1 6	7	1 8	2	4	3	6 8	5
Row B	8	4	2	3	6	5	9	1	7
Row C	1 5 6	3	1 5	9	1 8	7	4	2 6 8	2 8
Row D	1 2 5	1 5 7 8	4	5 7	1 3 8	9	6	2 5 8	2 3 8
Row E	1 3 5	1 5 7 8	1 3 5	2	4	6	1 7	5 **8**	9
Row F	1 2 5 6	1 5 6 7 8	9	5 7	1 3 8	1 8	1 7	4	2 3 8
Row G	1 3 5	1 5	1 3 5	4	9	2	8	7	6
Row H	7	9	6	1 8	5	1 8	2	3	4
Row I	4	2	8	6	7	3	5	9	1

The second pass for chaining uses the value 8 for the *head-link*, cell E-8. Chaining progression is as follows.

    link on the value 8 from E-8 to cell A-8,

      next link on the value 6 to cell A-2,

and link on 1 to cell A-4,

link on 8 to cell C-5,

link on 1 to cell C-3

The next linking value, 5, is equal to the *head-other* value and the Type D purging consideration is satisfied ("current-column", chain head row), so the value **5 can be purged from cell E-3**.

At this point end of chain is reached.

Chaining Values for Example 1

The chaining values for the second pass are shown in the puzzle grid below.

The chain establishes chaining values for six cells, and removes the candidate value 5 from cell E-3.

	Col 1	Col 2	Col 3	Col 4	Col 5	Col 6	Col 7	Col 8	Col 9
Row A	9	1	7	8	2	4	3	6	5
Row B	8	4	2	3	6	5	9	1	7
Row C	1 5 6	3	5	9	1	7	4	2 6 8	2 8
Row D	1 2 5	1 5 7 8	4		5 7	1 3 8	9	6	2 5 8	2 3 8
Row E	1 3 5	1 5 7 8	1 3		2	4		6	1 7	8	9
Row F	1 2 5 6	1 5 6 7 8	9		5 7	1 3 8	1 8	1 7	4	2 3 8
Row G	1 3 5	1 5	1 3 5	4	9	2	8	7	6
Row H	7	9	6	1 8	5	1 8	2	3	4
Row I	4	2	8	6	7	3	5	9	1

Example 2 for xy-chaining

For this example, the chain head is cell A-4. The first pass will use the value 4 for the *head-link* value. (The second pass would use 9 for the *head-link*.)

	Col 1	Col 2	Col 3	Col 4	Col 5	Col 6	Col 7	Col 8	Col 9
Row A	1 3 4 9	6	1 3 4 9	4 9	7	2	1 4	5	8
Row B	8	1 4 9	2	4 9	6	5	7	1 9	3
Row C	7	5	4 9	8	3	1	6	2 9	2 4

The first pass for chaining uses the value 4 for the *head-link*, cell A-4. Chaining progression is as follows.

link on the value 4 from A-4 to cell A-7,

next link on the value 1 to cell B-8

The next linking value, 9, is equal to the *head-other* value and the Type E purging consideration is satisfied (the cell in the "current row" and the same column as the chain head has the *head-other* value as a candidate), so the value **9 can be purged from cell B-4**.

Related Values Chaining

Three row partly-solved puzzle subset

This puzzle subset is used for the examples for Related Values. The chain head is cell C-9 and for the first chaining pass it is assumed to be 2. The chain links from cell C-9 to cell A-8 and on to A-4.

For the second chaining pass the head cell is assumed to be 4. The chain links from C-9 to C-7 and on to A-8.

	Col 1	Col 2	Col 3	Col 4	Col 5	Col 6	Col 7	Col 8	Col 9
A	1 4 9	1 2 4 9	7	1 5	1 5 9	3	8	1 2	6
B	1 3	1 3 8	6	2	1 8	4	9	7	5
C	1 9	2 8 9	5	7	1 8 9	6	1 4	3	2 4

Related Values Description

A Chaining Related Value is the value that a cell will have if the chain involved agrees with the solution to the puzzle.

For every cell there are three groups of directly related cells, those in the same row, the same column or the same box. Two directly related cells that are two-valued can be linked for chaining if they have a common candidate value.

For an xy-chain two chains may be analyzed, one for the chain head's smaller candidate value and the other for the chain head's larger candidate value. Initially it is unknown which chain will be "true" - will agree with the solution to the puzzle. For each of the two possible chains a set of Chaining Related Values can be developed. Each set of related values should be a table sized the same as the Sudoku puzzle (9 rows, 9 columns and 81 cells). Initially all of the related values are unknown (may be blank or zero). During chaining related values will be determined and put into the table. Note that the related values tables are not a copy of the puzzle cell values.

A cell with a known value before chaining is not involved in related values analysis.

The first step is to put the assumed value for the chain head into the related values table. When a chain link is determined, the link value (the value for the cell for chaining) is put into the table. As described in the following sections additional related values may be determined and put into the table.

Refer to the example puzzle subset above. During chaining consider a cell of interest, say cell A-1, with candidate values 1, 4 and 9. The following analysis can be performed :

- If any other cell in Row A has a related value that is 1, 4 or 9, then that candidate can't be true for cell A-1 for the chain being performed.
- If any other cell in Column 1 has a related value that is 1, 4 or 9, then that candidate can't be true for cell A-1 for the chain being performed.
- If any other cell in the containing box has a related value that is 1, 4 or 9, then that candidate can't be true for cell A-1 for the chain being performed.

For example: suppose that Cell A-1 has candidate values 1, 4 and 9, and during chaining cell A-8 is known to have a related value of 1, and cell C-1 is known to have a related value of 9. We can assign a chaining related value of 4 for Cell A-1 for the chain.

Derived Related Values

When a value is added to the Related Values Table, the related cells (in the same row, column or box) should be considered to determine additional Related Values. e.g. the cell for the value being added may have a two-valued related cell in the puzzle grid with that value as a candidate; if so that cell in the Related Values Table can be assigned the cell's other candidate value as a Derived Related Value.

Related Values Conflicts

If a row, column, or box in the Related Values Table has some value two or more times then a Chaining Conflict has occurred. This conflict is handled the same as a Type G xy-chaining conflict - the *head-link* value is purged from the chain head cell. An example is shown below in the Section "Example for Conflict in Related Values".

Possibility of Solution

There is a possible big payoff for the related values analysis: related values may be determined for all unknown cells. When this occurs the puzzle is solved, that is the chaining being performed assumed a value for the chain head which leads to the solution to the puzzle ("the chain is true"). **Each related value solves the corresponding puzzle cell.**

Analyzing the chains for both passes

A more likely, smaller, benefit is that one or more corresponding cells in the two related values tables have the same value. This means that no matter which of the two possible values the chain head takes on, the related value solves the corresponding puzzle cell. **The puzzle cell should be set to the related value.** Note that the cell solved is not part of the chain, is not a chain link.

Related Values Determination and Longer Chains

Extended logic for additional chain links and longer chains is described in the section *Longer chains with Related Values*.

Related Values Chaining Example

This detailed example for Related Values uses the partly-solved puzzle subset shown above. For the chain head, cell C-9, two chains will be analyzed with a description of chaining related values. Pass 1 is for the chain starting with the cell's smaller candidate value, and Pass 2 is for the chain starting with the cell's larger candidate value.

Example Pass 1

The chain head is cell C-9, and is assumed to be 2. The chain links from cell C-9 to cell A-8 and on to A-4. For this three-cell chain we have these Considerations for related values:

1. cell C-9 is assumed to be 2 and is assigned Related Value 2
2. consequently cell A-8 would be 1 and is assigned Related Value 1
3. cell A-4 would be 5 and is assigned Related Value 5
4. the cells in row C other than C-9 may not have 2 as a candidate value
5. cells in row A other than A-4 and A-8 may not have value 1 or 5
6. cells in column 9 other than C-9 may not have 2
7. cells in column 8 other than A-8 may not have 1
8. cells in column 4 other than A-4 may not have 5
9. cells in the third box other than C-9 and A-8 may not have have 1 or 2
10. cells in the second box other than A-4 may not have 5

Additional related values, part 1

- Consideration (2) above has an implication for cell A-2 - it is now the only cell in row A that can take on candidate value 2 for the puzzle solution when the chain is true. So the related value for the cell is set to 2. As cell A-2 is not a link of the chain, this consideration is additional information that may help solve the puzzle.
- Consider (5) above regarding cell A-5 - the cell's candidates are 1, 5 and 9 so the related value for the cell is set to 9.
- Consider (9) above regarding cell C-7 - the cell's candidates are 1 and 4 so the related value for the cell is set to 4.

The additional related value considerations for part 1 are:

11. cell A-2 is assigned Related Value 2
12. cell A-5 is assigned Related Value 9
13. cell C-7 is assigned Related Value 4
14. the cells in row A other than A-2 and A-5 may not have 2 or 9 as candidate values (related to (5) above)
15. cells in row C other than C-7 may not have 4 (related to (4) above)
16. cells in column 2 other than A-2 may not have 2
17. cells in column 5 other than A-5 may not have 9
18. cells in column 7 other than C-7 may not have 4
19. cells in the first box other than A-2 may not have 2
20. cells in the second box other than A-5 may not have 9 (related to (10) above)

21. cells in the third box other than C-7 may not have 4 (related to (9) above)

Additional related values, part 2

- Consider both (5) and (14) above regarding cell A-1 - the cell's candidates are 1, 4 and 9, so the chaining related value for the cell is 4.

The related value considerations can be extended to include:

22. cell A-1 is assigned Related Value 4
23. the cells in row A other than A-1 may not have 4 as a candidate value (related to (5) above)
24. cells in column 1 other than A-1 may not have 4
25. cells in the first box other than A-1 may not have 4 (related to (19) above

Here are the seven chaining related values for pass 1 shown in a puzzle grid. The cells that are known for the example are indicated with an "*" character. The cells shown as blank do not have an assigned related value.

Related values for pass 1, cell C-9 = 2

	Col 1	Col 2	Col 3	Col 4	Col 5	Col 6	Col 7	Col 8	Col 9
Row A	4	2	*	5	9	*	*	1	*
Row B			*	*		*	*	*	*
Row C			*	*		*	4	*	2

Example Pass 2

This is the second chain for head cell C-9. The chain head, cell C-9, is assumed to be the cell's larger value, 4. The chain links from cell C-9 to cell C-7 and on to A-8.

For this chain we have these Considerations for related values:

1. cell C-9 is assumed to be 4 and is assigned Related Value 4
2. cell C-7 would be 1 and is assigned Related Value 1
3. cell A-8 would be 2 and is assigned Related Value 2
4. the cells in row C other than C-9 and C-7 may not have 1 or 4 as a candidate value
5. cells in row A other than A-8 may not have 2 as a candidate value
6. cells in column 9 other than C-9 may not have the value 4
7. cells in column 7 other than C-7 may not have 1
8. cells in column 8 other than A-8 may not have 2
9. cells in the containing box other than C-9, C-7 and A-8 may not have 1, 2 or 4

22

Additional related values, part 1

- Consideration (4) above has an implication for cell C-1 - the cell's candidates are 1 and 9 so the chaining related value for the cell would be 9. This consideration may help solve the puzzle.
- Consider (5) above regarding cell C-2 - it is now the only cell in it's box with a candidate value of 2, so the related value for the cell is set to 2.

The additional related value considerations for part 1 are:

10. cell C-1 is assigned Related Value 9
11. cell C-2 is assigned Related Value 2
12. the cells in row C other than C-1 and C-2 may not have 2 or 9 as candidate values (related to (4) above)
13. cells in column 1 other than C-1 may not have the value 9
14. cells in column 2 other than C-2 may not have 2
15. cells in the first box other than C-1 and C-2 may not have 2 or 9

Additional related values, part 2

- Consider (15) above regarding cell A-5 - it is now the only cell in it's row with a candidate value of 9, so the related value for the cell would be 9.
- Now consider cell A-4 - the only cell in it's row with a candidate value of 5, so the related value for the cell would be 5.
- Consider both (4) and (12) above regarding cell C-5 - the cell's candidates are 1, 8 and 9, so the related value for the cell would be 8.
- Now consider cell B-5, which has candidates 1 and 8, so the related value would be 1.
- Consider cell B-1, which has candidates 1 and 3, the related value would be 3.
- Consider cell B-2, which has candidates 1, 3 and 8, the related value would be 8.

The related value considerations can be extended to include:

16. cell A-5 is assigned Related Value 9
17. cell A-4 is assigned Related Value 5
18. cell C-5 is assigned Related Value 8
19. cell B-5 is assigned Related Value 1
20. cell B-1 is assigned Related Value 3
21. cell B-2 is assigned Related Value 8
22. the cells in row A other than A-4 and A-5 may not have 5 or 9 (related to (5) above)
23. cells in row B other than B-1, B-2 and B-5 may not have 1, 3 or 8
24. cells in row C other than C-5 may not have 8 (related to (4) and (12) above
25. cells in column 1 other than B-1 may not have 3 (related to (13) above)
26. cells in column 2 other than B-2 may not have 8 (related to (14) above)
27. cells in column 4 other than A-4 may not have 5
28. cells in column 5 other than A-5, C-5 and B-5 may not have 1, 8 or 9
29. cells in the first box other than B-1 and B-2 may not have 3 or 8 (related to (15)

above)

30. cells in the second box other than A-4, A-5, B-5 and C-5 may not have 1, 5, 8 or 9

Here are the eleven related values shown in a puzzle grid. The cells that are known for the example are indicated with an "*" character.

Related values for pass 2, cell C-9 = 4

	Col 1	Col 2	Col 3	Col 4	Col 5	Col 6	Col 7	Col 8	Col 9
Row A			*	5	9	*	*	2	*
Row B	3	8	*	*	1	*	*	*	*
Row C	9	2	*	*	8	*	1	*	4

Analyzing Related Values for both chains

The preceding sections describe both passes for chaining on the example puzzle subset. For the two sets of related values there are two corresponding cells that have the same value. For both values of the chain head the related value for cell A-4 is 5; and the related value for cell A-5 is 9. **So these two puzzle cells are solved.** Note that the underlying basic chaining logic didn't solve anything. Refer to *Related values for cell C-9 = 2* and *Related values for cell C-9 = 4*.

Longer chains with Related Values

Related values considerations can enlarge the set of chaining link candidates, leading to longer chains. Referring to the example puzzle subset shown below, consider a chain with head cell C-2 having the assumed value of 4.

The chain links on the value 4 from cell C-2 to cell C-9, then links on the value 5 to Cell C-4. The chain has three linked cells.

Now consider cell C-6, which initially has four candidate values, {1, 2, 4, 5}. Using related value considerations, the cell's possible chaining candidates are only the values {1, 2} (the related values of 4 and 5 have been assigned to cells C-2 and C-9). So cell C-6 is a chain link candidate, and we can link on the value 1 from cell C-4 to cell C-6.

As cell C-3 initially had candidate values {1, 2, 3, 4, 5}, it's possible chaining candidates are only the values {2, 3}. So we can link on the value 2 from cell C-6 to cell C-3. Thus we have a longer chain with five linked cells.

Longer chain example

	Col 1	Col 2	Col 3	Col 4	Col 5	Col 6	Col 7	Col 8	Col 9
A	1 2 4 5	1 2 4 6 8	9	1 2 5 8	1 2 4 8	3	1 4 5 6	1 4 6	7
B	1 3 4 5	1 3 4 6 8	1 3 4 5 8	9	1 4 7 8	1 4 5 7 8	1 4 5 6	1 3 4 6	2
C	7	3 **4**	1 2 3 4 5	1 5	6	1 2 4 5	9	8	4 5

Example for Conflict in Related Values

This example for chaining related values has a conflict for the related values. For this example the chain head is cell A-7. The second chaining pass uses the value 4 for the *head-link*.

	Col 1	Col 2	Col 3		Col 4	Col 5	Col 6		Col 7	Col 8	Col 9
Row A	1 3 4	6	1 3 4		9	7	2		1 **4**	5	8
Row B	8	1 9	2		4	6	5		7	1 9	3
Row C	7	5	4 9		8	3	1		6	2 9	2 4
Row D	1 4 9	1 2 4	7		1 5	1 5 9	3		8	1 2	6
Row E	1 3	1 3 8	6		2	1 8	4		9	7	5
Row F	1 9	2 8	5		7	1 8 9	6		1 4	3	2 4
Row G	6	1 3 4	1 3 4		1 5	1 2 5	7		2 3	8	9
Row H	2	7	8		3	4	9		5	6	1
Row I	5	1 3 9	1 3 9		6	1 2	8		2 3	4	7

Here are the chaining related values for the second pass shown in a puzzle grid. The cells that are known for the example are indicated with an "*" character. The cells shown as blank do not have an assigned related value.

Related values for second pass

	Col 1	Col 2	Col 3	Col 4	Col 5	Col 6	Col 7	Col 8	Col 9
Row A	1	*	3	*	*	*	4	*	*
Row B	*	9	*	*	*	*	*	1	*
Row C	*	*	4	*	*	*	*	9	2
Row D	4		*	5	9	*	*	2	*
Row E	3	8	*	*	1	*	*	*	*
Row F	9	2	*	*	8	*	1	*	4
Row G	*		3	1	5	*	2	*	*
Row H	*	*	*	*	*	*	*	*	*
Row I	*	1		*	2	*	3	*	*

Note the conflict for two 3's in Column 3. The conflict is handled the same as a <u>Type G</u> xy-chaining conflict, by purging the *head-link* value from the chain head cell. So **cell A-7 can be set to 1**.

After purging the solution to the puzzle is straightforward. The solution is shown below.

Puzzle Solution

	Col 1	Col 2	Col 3	Col 4	Col 5	Col 6	Col 7	Col 8	Col 9
Row A	3	6	4	9	7	2	1	5	8
Row B	8	1	2	4	6	5	7	9	3
Row C	7	5	9	8	3	1	6	2	4
Row D	4	2	7	5	9	3	8	1	6
Row E	1	3	6	2	8	4	9	7	5
Row F	9	8	5	7	1	6	4	3	2
Row G	6	4	3	1	5	7	2	8	9
Row H	2	7	8	3	4	9	5	6	1
Row I	5	9	1	6	2	8	3	4	7

Related Values Chaining - the Payoff

Related values chaining can solve puzzles that ordinary xy-chaining cannot. The example from the previous section for basic xy-chaining is analyzed using related values chaining ("enhanced xy-chaining").

Example Puzzle

The example puzzle ("Example 1 for xy-chaining") is repeated here. The chain head is cell E-8. The first pass for chaining would use the value 5 for the *head-link* value. The second pass uses 8 for the *head-link*. The second pass is described for the example.

	Col 1	Col 2	Col 3	Col 4	Col 5	Col 6	Col 7	Col 8	Col 9
Row A	9	1 6	7	1 8	2	4	3	6 8	5
Row B	8	4	2	3	6	5	9	1	7
Row C	1 5 6	3	1 5	9	1 8	7	4	2 6 8	2 8
Row D	1 2 5	1 5 7 8	4		5 7	1 3 8	9	6	2 5 8	2 3 8
Row E	1 3 5	1 5 7 8	1 3 5	2	4	6	1 7	5 8	9
Row F	1 2 5 6	1 5 6 7 8	9	5 7	1 3 8	1 8	1 7	4	2 3 8
Row G	1 3 5	1 5	1 3 5	4	9	2	8	7	6
Row H	7	9	6	1 8	5	1 8	2	3	4
Row I	4	2	8	6	7	3	5	9	1

The second pass for chaining uses the value 8 for the *head-link*, cell E-8. Chaining progression is as follows.

link on the value 8 from E-8 to cell A-8

At this point the related values for the chain head cell (E-8) and for the second cell (A-8) are analyzed. The following related values can be assigned:

1. cell E-8 related value 8
2. cell A-8 related value 6
3. cell A-2 related value 1
4. cell C-8 related value 2
5. cell A-4 related value 8

29

6. cell G-2 related value 5
7. cell C-3 related value 5
8. cell D-8 related value 5
9. cell C-9 related value 8
10. cell H-4 related value 1
11. cell C-5 related value 1
12. cell E-2 related value 7
13. cell C-1 related value 6
14. cell D-4 related value 7
15. cell H-6 related value 8
16. cell D-2 related value 8
17. cell E-7 related value 1
18. cell F-4 related value 5
19. cell F-6 related value 1
20. cell D-5 related value 3
21. cell F-2 related value 6
22. cell E-3 related value 3
23. cell F-7 related value 7
24. cell F-1 related value 2
25. cell F-5 related value 8
26. cell D-9 related value 2
27. cell E-1 related value 5
28. cell G-3 related value 1
29. cell D-1 related value 1
30. cell F-9 related value 3
31. cell G-1 related value 3

The related values are shown below. Cells with a known value before the chaining starts are shown as "*".

Related values are determined for all unknown puzzle cells, each related value solves the corresponding puzzle cell. **The puzzle is solved.**

Related Values for enhanced xy-chaining

	Col 1	Col 2	Col 3	Col 4	Col 5	Col 6	Col 7	Col 8	Col 9
Row A	*	1	*	8	*	*	*	6	*
Row B	*	*	*	*	*	1	*	*	*
Row C	6	*	5	*	1	*	*	2	8
Row D	1	8	*	7	3	*	*	5	2
Row E	5	7	3	*	*	*	1	8	*
Row F	2	6	*	5	8	1	7	*	3
Row G	3	5	1	*	*	*	*	*	*
Row H	*	*	*	1	*	8	*	*	*
Row I	*	*	*	*	*	*	*	*	*

Tree Chaining

Tree Chaining using Related Values is described using the example puzzle shown below.

Tree Chaining example subset

For the Chain Tree example the chain head is cell B-8. The second chaining pass is considered and the *head-link* value is **4**.

	Col 1	Col 2	Col 3	Col 4	Col 5	Col 6	Col 7	Col 8	Col 9
Row A	4 5	6	3	8	2	1 4 5	7 9	7 9	1 4 5
Row B	7	4 8	5 8	1 3 4 5	1 3 5	9	2	1 4	6
Row C	2	1	9	4 5 6	5 6	7	3	8	4 5

Description of Tree Chaining

A Chain Tree is formed when a cell in a chain links to two or more cells, giving a multi-branched chain. Chain Trees can have more than two branches.

A Chain Tree can be found in the example puzzle. The chain head is cell B-8, and is assumed to be 4. The chain's first branch links from cell B-8 to cell B-2, then on to B-3 and finally A-1. The second branch links from cell B-8 to C-9 and then to C-5. This chain tree has the following related value considerations:

1. cell B-8 is assumed to be 4 and is assigned Related Value 4
2. cell B-2 would be 8 and is assigned Related Value 8
3. cell B-3 would be 5 and is assigned Related Value 5
4. cell A-1 would be 4 and is assigned Related Value 4
5. for the second branch, cell C-9 would be 5 and is assigned Related Value 5
6. cell C-5 would be 6 and is assigned Related Value 6
7. the cells in row B other than B-2, B-3 and B-8 may not have 4, 5 or 8 as candidate values
8. cells in row A other than A-1 may not have the value 4
9. cells in row C other than C-5 and C-9 may not have 5 or 6
10. cells in column 1 other than A-1 may not have 4
11. cells in column 2 other than B-2 may not have 8
12. cells in column 3 other than B-3 may not have 5
13. cells in column 5 other than C-5 may not have 6
14. cells in column 8 other than B-8 may not have 4

15. cells in column 9 other than C-9 may not have 5
16. cells in the first box other than A-1, B-2 and B-3 may not have have 4, 5 or 8
17. cells in the second box other than C-5 may not have have 6
18. cells in the third box other than B-8 and C-9 may not have have 4 or 5

Additional related values

- Considerations (1) and (5) above have an implication for cell A-9 - the cell's candidates are 1, 4 and 5 so it's related value would be 1.
- Considerations (5) and (6) above have an implication for cell C-4 - the cell's candidates are 4, 5 and 6 so it's related value would be 4.
- With these two additional related values determined, there is an implication for cell A-6 - it's candidates are 1, 4 and 5, so it's related value would be 5.

The additional related value considerations are:

19. cell A-9 is assigned Related Value 1
20. cell C-4 is assigned Related Value 4
21. cell A-6 is assigned Related Value 5
22. the cells in row A other than A-6 and A-9 may not have the value 1 or 5 (related to (8) above)
23. cells in row C other than C-4 may not have 4 (related to (9) above)
24. cells in column 4 other than C-4 may not have 4
25. cells in column 6 other than A-6 may not have 5
26. cells in column 9 other than A-9 may not have 1 (related to (15) above)
27. cells in the second box other than A-6 and C-4 may not have 4 or 5 (related to (17) above)
28. cells in the third box other than A-9 may not have 1 (related to (18) above)

Here are the 9 related values determined, shown in a puzzle grid. The cells that are known for the example are indicated with an "*" character.

Related values for Chain Tree

	Col 1	Col 2	Col 3	Col 4	Col 5	Col 6	Col 7	Col 8	Col 9
Row A	4	*	*	*	*	5			1
Row B	*	8	5			*	*	4	*
Row C	*	*	*	4	6	*	*	*	5

Chaining Methods, Corners and Exocet

Several Chaining Methods are described, all of which use Tree Chaining and Related Values. For these Chaining Methods Type A, B, C, D and E chaining purging are not performed. Type F and Type G chaining purging are described for each Method. (Chaining purging is described in the Section *xy-chaining*.) The Methods are:

- Three values Chaining
- Four values Chaining
- Five values Chaining
- Dual Triple Chaining

Also the *Corners Technique*, which doesn't use chaining, is described.

And the non-chaining Technique named *Exocet* is described.

Several non-chaining Techniques named "BigFish" are described in *Appendix A*.

The non-chaining Techniques named "Two Segments" are described in *Appendix B*.

Three Values Chaining

Three values Chaining is a variation on xy-chaining. The chain head cell is chosen as a three-valued cell. Three chains will be formed, one for each candidate value of the head cell. For each chain a second cell will be chosen the same way as for xy-chaining. Note that the second and subsequent cells are two-valued.

Three values chaining performs three passes, one for each chain, using the following values for the chain head :

Chain Head value for each pass

Pass	Chain head
1	low value
2	high value
3	middle value

This differs from xy-chaining in that :

- the chain head cell has **three** candidate values, three chains will be analyzed
- if a Type F or Type G chaining conflict occurs, the head cell is purged as described below

For Related Values, three sets of values are used, one for each pass.

Conflict Considerations

If there are conflict(s) the chain head can be purged according to the pass(es) that have a conflict.

Purging for Three values Chaining

Pass	Chain head
1	remove low value
2	remove high value
3	remove middle value

Example for Three values Chaining

For this example, the chain head is cell D-3 and the triple value is {2, 7, 9}. Up to three chaining passes may be performed. The first pass will use the value 2 for the chain head.

	Col 1	Col 2	Col 3	Col 4	Col 5	Col 6	Col 7	Col 8	Col 9
A	7 9	3	7 9	8	6	5	2 4	2 4	1
B	2	1	5	3	4	7	6	8 9	8 9
C	4	8	6	9	2	1	3	5	7
D	7 9	2 4 5 9	2 7 9	6	8	3 4	1	2 3 9	2 5 9
E	6	2 5	3	1 5	1 7	9	8	2 7	4
F	1	4 5 9	8	4 5	3 7	2	5 7 9	3 6 7 9	5 6 9
G	3	7	1 2	1 2 4	9	8	2 4 5	2 4 6	2 5 6
H	8	2 9	4	7	5	6	2 9	1	3
I	5	6	1 2 9	1 2 4	1 3	3 4	2 4 7 9	2 4 7 8 9	2 8 9

The first pass for chaining uses the value 2 for the chain head, cell D-3. Chaining progression is:

link on the value 2 from D-3 to cell E-2,

   then link on the value 5 to cell D-2,
   then link on the value 9 to cell D-1,
   then link on the value 7 to cell A-1,
   then link on the value 9 to cell A-3

Note that the value of cell D-2 before chaining starts is {2, 4, 5, 9}. When the Related value of 2 is set for the cell D-3, the chaining candidate values for cell D-2 are reduced to{4, 5, 9}; subsequently the related value of 4 is set for cell D-6 (see Note below) and the chaining candidate values for cell D-2 are reduced to {5, 9}, thus the cell can be a chain link as it has two possible candidate values.

Related Values are determined for all 36 unknown puzzle cells - **the chain solves the puzzle**.

Note for cell D-6

   First cell D-3 is assigned related value 2;

      then cell E-2 can be assigned related value 5,
         and cell E-4 can be assigned related value 1,
         and cell E-5 can be assigned related value 7,
         and cell F-5 can be assigned related value 3,
         and cell D-6 can be assigned related value 4

The related values are shown below. Cells with a known value before the chaining starts are shown as "*".

Related Values for pass 1, cell D-3 = 2

	Col 1	Col 2	Col 3	Col 4	Col 5	Col 6	Col 7	Col 8	Col 9
Row A	9	*	7	*	*	*	2	4	*
Row B	*	*	*	*	*	*	*	8	9
Row C	*	*	*	*	*	*	*	*	*
Row D	7	9	2	*	*	4	*	3	5
Row E	*	5	*	1	7	*	*	2	*
Row F	*	4	*	5	3	*	7	9	6
Row G	*	*	1	4	*	*	5	6	2
Row H	*	2	*	*	*	*	9	*	*
Row I	*	*	9	2	1	3	4	7	8

Related Values are determined for all unknown puzzle cells, each related value solves the corresponding puzzle cell. **The puzzle is solved.**

Four / Five Values chaining

These Chaining Methods are similar to Three Values Chaining. The chain head cell is chosen as a four- or five- valued cell, and four or five chains will be analyzed. Chain progression (linking) from the first cell onward is the same as for xy-chaining. The second and subsequent cells are two-valued.

These methods perform four or five passes choosing each candidate value for the chain head. The candidate values are designated as "A" for the low value, "B" for the next to lowest value, "C" for the next higher value, "D" for the next higher value and, for Five Values Chaining "E" for the high value. (For Four Values Chaining, "D" is the highest value.)

For each pass the following values are used for the chain head :

Chain Head value to use

Pass	Four Values	Five Values
1	value "A"	value "A"
2	value "D"	value "E"
3	value "B"	value "B"
4	value "C"	value "C"
5	N/A	value "D"

This differs from xy-chaining in that :

- the chain head cell has **4** or **5** candidate values, **4** or **5** chains will be analyzed
- if a Type F or Type G chaining conflict occurs, the head cell is purged as described below

For Related Values, 4 or 5 sets of values are used, one for each pass.

Conflict Considerations

If there are conflict(s) the chain head can be purged according to the pass(es) that have a conflict.

Purging for Pass(es) with conflict

Pass	Four Values	Five Values
1	remove value "A"	remove value "A"
2	remove value "D"	remove value "E"
3	remove value "B"	remove value "B"
4	remove value "C"	remove value "C"
5	N/A	remove value "D"

Example for Four Values Chaining

For this example, the chain head is cell A-5 and the "quad" value is {1, 2, 3, 8}. Up to four chaining passes may be performed. The passes will use values 1, 8, 2 and 3 for the chain head.

	Col 1	Col 2	Col 3	Col 4	Col 5	Col 6	Col 7	Col 8	Col 9
A	3 4 6 / 8	1 2 3 / 4	1 2 3 / 4 6	1 2 5 / 6 8	1 2 3 / 8	1 2 3 / 5 6 8	1 2 3 / 4	7	9
B	3 6 9	1 2 3 / 9	1 2 3 / 6	1 2 6 / 7	1 2 3 / 7	4	1 2 3	5	8
C	3 4 8	5	7	1 2 8	9	1 2 3 / 8	6	1 2 3 / 4	1 2 3 / 4
D	3 4 5	8	9	1 2 4 / 5	6	1 2 5	1 2 3 / 4 5	2 3 4	7
E	2	7	1 3 4 / 5 6	1 4 5 / 8	1 8	9	1 3 4 / 5 8	1 3 4 / 6 8	1 3 4 / 5
F	4 5 6	1 4	1 4 5 / 6	3	1 2 7 / 8	1 2 5 / 7 8	9	1 2 4 / 6 8	1 2 4 / 5
G	3 5 7 / 9	2 3 9	2 3 5	1 2 7 / 8 9	4	1 2 3 / 7 8	1 2 3 / 5 7 8	1 2 3 / 8	6
H	3 4 7	6	8	1 2 7	5	1 2 3 / 7	1 2 3 / 4 7	9	1 2 3 / 4
I	1	2 3 4 / 9	2 3 4 / 5	2 6 7 / 8 9	2 3 7 / 8	2 3 6 / 7 8	2 3 4 / 5 7 8	2 3 4 / 8	2 3 4 / 5

For this example, the quad value is {1, 2, 3, 8}. The chain head is cell A-5.

The first pass for chaining, which uses the value 1 for the chain head, completes error-free.

The second pass uses the value 8 for the chain head and links from cell A-5 to cell E-5 - the chain is short. A chaining conflict for related values is determined. Per *"Purging for Pass(es) with conflict"* above, the candidate value 8 can be removed from the chain head cell.

All of the related values are shown below. Note conflicts for :

- two 2's in row G, in the same box
- two 7's in row H
- two 5's in column 3

41

Related Values for pass 2, cell A-5 = 8

	Col 1	Col 2	Col 3	Col 4	Col 5	Col 6	Col 7	Col 8	Col 9
Row A	.	.	.	5	8	.	.	.	.
Row B	.	.	.	.	7	.	.	.	.
Row C	8	.	.	2	.	3	.	1	4
Row D	3	.	.	4	.	5	1	2	.
Row E	.	.	5	8	1	.	4	6	3
Row F	.	.	.	.	2	7	.	8	5
Row G	7	2	2	.	.	.	.	3	.
Row H	.	.	.	7	.	2	7	.	1
Row I	.	9	5	.	3	.	.	4	2

Dual Triple Chaining

Dual Triple Chaining is a variation on xy-chaining. Instead of starting with a single cell being selected for the chain head, two cells are chosen to be the chain head and the chain's second cell:

- the first cell can be any three-valued cell
- the second cell can be any other three-valued cell

Chain progression (linking) from the second cell onward is the same as for xy-chaining.

Whereas xy-chaining performs two passes, one for each value of the chain head cell, Dual Triple chaining performs nine passes using the following values for the chain head and the second cell, where the chain head's three candidate values are designated as "A" for it's low value, "B" for it's medium value and "C" for it's high value, and the second cell's three candidate values are designated as "D" for it's low value, "E" for it's medium value and "F" for it's high value:

Cell values for each pass

Pass	Chain head	Second cell
1	"A"	"D"
2	"A"	"F"
3	"C"	"F"
4	"C"	"D"
5	"A"	"E"
6	"C"	"E"
7	"B"	"D"
8	"B"	"F"
9	"B"	"E"

This differs from xy-chaining in that :

- the chain head cell and the second cell have **three values**, nine chains will be analyzed
- the chain head and the second cell may or may not be in the same row, column or box
- the candidate values of the chain head and the second cell may be unrelated
- Type F purge logic is not performed
- if a Type G chaining conflict occurs, purging of the chain head and/or the second cell is performed as described below

For Related Values, **nine(*)** sets of related values will be used, one for each pass. When processing completes, if for some puzzle cell the same related value is determined for all(*) passes the cell is solved and will be set to the related value.

Conflict Considerations

(*) If there are conflicts, the set of related values corresponding to the conflict(s) are disregarded.

If there are eight conflicts both the chain head and the second cell can be purged according to the pass that was conflict free.

If there are 3 conflicts a purge may be possible for the chain head or the second cell based on which passes have conflicts, as shown below.

If there are 4 - 7 conflicts purge(s) may be possible for the chain head and/or the second cell based on which passes have conflicts.

Purging for 3 - 7 conflicts

Passes with conflicts	Chain head	Second cell
1, 2 and 5	value "A"	no purge
3, 4 and 6	value "C"	no purge
7, 8 and 9	value "B"	no purge
1, 4 and 7	no purge	value "D"
2, 3 and 8	no purge	value "F"
5, 6 and 9	no purge	value "E"

For example, if there are conflicts for passes 1, 2, 4, 5 and 7 then two purges can be performed: candidate value "A" can be purged for the chain head, and candidate value "D" can be purged for the second cell. An example puzzle is presented.

Dual-Triple chaining example

	Col 1	Col 2	Col 3	Col 4	Col 5	Col 6	Col 7	Col 8	Col 9
A	1	3 4 9	3 8 9	2	7 8 9	3 5 9	4 5	3 6 7	3 4 5 6
B	2 3 9	6	5	1 3 7 9	1 7 9	4	8	1 2 3 7	1 2 3
C	2 3 4 8	7	2 3 8	1 3 5 8	1 5 8	6	9	1 2 3	1 2 3 4 5
D	2 3 6 7 8	1 2 3	4	1 5 6 7	1 2 5 6 7	1 5	1 2 3 5	9	1 2 3 5 6 8
E	2 3 6 9	5	1 2 3 9	4	2 6 9	8	7	1 2 3 6	1 2 3 6
F	2 6 7 8 9	1 2 9	1 2 7 8 9	5 6 7 9	3	1 5 9	1 2 5	4	1 2 5 6 8
G	2 3 4 5 7 9	1 2 3 4 9	1 2 3 7 9	1 3 5 8 9	1 4 5 8 9	1 3 5 9	6	1 2 3	1 2 3 4
H	3 4 9	8	1 3 9	1 3 6 9	1 4 6 9	2	1 3 4	5	7
I	2 3 5	1 2 3 4	6	1 3 5	1 4 5	7	1 2 3 4	8	9

For this example the chain head is cell A-2 and it's value is { 3, 4, 9 }. The second cell in the chain is F-6 with value { 1, 5, 9 }. As designated above these chaining values are:

"A" = 3, "B" = 4, "C" = 9; "D" = 1, "E" = 5, "F" = 9.

The first pass for chaining, which uses the value 3 for the chain head and 1 for the second cell, results in a chaining conflict (either the value 3 is incorrect for cell A-2, and-or the value 1 is incorrect for cell F-6.)

The second pass which uses the value 3 for the chain head and the value 9 for the second cell also results in a chaining conflict. (together these two values are incorrect).

The third pass which uses the value 9 for both the chain head and the second cell completes error-free.

The fourth pass, which uses the value 9 for the chain head and the value 1 for the second cell results in a chaining conflict.

And the fifth pass, which uses the value 3 for the chain head and the value 5 for the second cell results in a chaining conflict.

The sixth pass, which uses the value 9 for the chain head and the value 5 for the second cell completes error-free.

The seventh pass, which uses the value 4 for the chain head and the value 1 for the second cell results in a chaining conflict.

The eighth pass, which uses the value 4 for the chain head and the value 9 for the second cell completes error-free.

And the ninth pass, which uses the value 4 for the chain head and the value 5 for the second cell completes error-free.

Referring to *Purging for 3 - 7 conflicts* above, the candidate value "A" can be purged for the chain head, and candidate value "D" can be purged for the second cell. i.e. **cell A-2 can be set to { 4, 9 }** and **cell F-6 can be set to { 5, 9 }.**

Corners Technique

The *Corners Technique* considers a single candidate value and looks for a pattern across multiple cells in up to four boxes that form the corners of a rectangle. If the pattern is matched the candidate value can be removed from one corner cell. Chaining is not involved.

For the <u>first rectangle corner</u>, choose a cell, call it *cell1*, and call it's box *box a*, that has multiple candidate values, and select one of it's candidate values, call it *edge value*, for which:

A. the *edge value* appears in it's row outside of *box a*,

B. the *edge value* appears in it's column outside of *box a*

Next <u>Check for the second corner</u>: check for another box, call it *box b*, that shares the same columns for which:

C. *edge value* appears two or more times in *box b*,

D. a cell in *box b*, in *cell1*'s column, call it *cell2*, satisfies either A1 - A4 or B1 - B5 :

- ■ A1 *cell2* has *edge value* as a candidate,

- ■ A2 {*cell2*'s row segment and *cell2*'s column segment} have the only cells in *box b* with *edge value* as a candidate,

- ■ A3 the *edge value* appears in *cell2*'s row outside of *box b*,

- ■ A4 *cell2*'s row segment has two or more cells with *edge value* as a candidate

- ■ B1 *cell2* does not have *edge value* as a candidate,

- ■ B2 {*cell2*'s row segment and *cell2*'s column segment} have the only cells in *box b* with "edge value as a candidate,

- ■ B3 the *edge value* appears in *cell2*'s row outside of *box b*,

- ■ B4 *cell2*'s row segment has one or more cells with *edge value* as a candidate,

- ■ B5 *cell2*'s column segment has one or more cells with *edge value* as a candidate

E. with either A1-A4 or B1-B5 satisfied, *cell1* may be purged if there is another box, call it *box x*, that shares *cell2*'s row for which:

- ■ *edge value* appears two or more times in *box x*,

- ■ a cell in *box x*, in *cell2*'s row, call it *cellx*, satisfies C1 and C2 :

  - ● C1 *cellx* has *edge value* as a candidate,

  - ● C2 in *cellx*'s column *edge value* appears two times, in *cell1*'s row and in *cellx*'s row

- ■ with the above satisfied, purge *edge value* from *cell1*

F. <u>Check for the third corner</u>: with either A1-A4 or B1-B5 satisfied, look for another box, call it *box c*, that shares *cell2*'s row for which:

- ■ *edge value* appears two or more times in *box c*,

- ■ a cell in *box c*, in *cell2*'s row, call it *cell3*, satisfies either D1 - D4 or E1 - E5 :
  - • D1 *cell3* has *edge value* as a candidate,
  - • D2 {*cell3*'s row segment and *cell3*'s column segment} have the only cells in *box c* with *edge value* as a candidate,
  - • D3 the *edge value* appears in *cell3*'s column outside of *box c*,
  - • D4 *cell3*'s column segment has two or more cells with *edge value* as a candidate
  - • E1 *cell3* does not have *edge value* as a candidate,
  - • E2 {*cell3*'s row segment and *cell3*'s column segment} have the only cells in *box c* with *edge value* as a candidate,
  - • E3 the *edge value* appears in *cell3*'s column outside of *box c*,
  - • E4 *cell3*'s row segment has one or more cells with *edge value* as a candidate,
  - • E5 *cell3*'s column segment has one or more cells with *edge value* as a candidate

- ■ with either D1-D4 or E1-E5 satisfied, *cell1* may be purged if there is another box, call it *box y*, that shares *cell3*'s column for which:
  - • *edge value* appears two or more times in *box y*,
  - • a cell in *box y*, in *cell3*'s column, call it *celly*, satisfies F1 and F2 :
    - ♦ F1 *celly* has *edge value* as a candidate,
    - ♦ F2 in *celly*'s row *edge value* appears two times, in *cell1*'s column and in *celly*'s column
  - • with the above satisfied, purge *edge value* from *cell1*

- ■ *Check for the fourth corner*: with either D1-D4 or E1-E5 satisfied, check the cell in *cell1*'s row and *cell3*'s column, call it *cell4*, to determine if :
  - • *edge value* appears two or more times in *cell4*'s box,
  - • *cell4* satisfies either G1 - G3 or H1 - H4 :
    - ♦ G1 *cell4* has *edge value* as a candidate,
    - ♦ G2 {*cell4*'s row segment and *cell4*'s column segment} have the only cells in *cell4*'s box with *edge value* as a candidate,
    - ♦ G3 *cell4*'s row segment has two or more cells with *edge value* as a candidate
    - ♦ H1 *cell4* does not have *edge value* as a candidate,
    - ♦ H2 {*cell4*'s row segment and *cell4*'s column segment} have the only cells in *cell4*'s box with "edge value as a candidate,
    - ♦ H3 *cell4*'s row segment has one or more cells with *edge value* as a candidate,
    - ♦ H4 *cell4*'s column segment has one or more cells with "edge value" as a candidate
  - • with either G1-G3 or H1-H4 satisfied, purge *edge value* from *cell1*

Example for Corners

An example is described, using the partly solved example puzzle below.

For this example the *first rectangle corner* ("*cell1*") is cell C-8, in box 3, it's value is { 2, 3, 4 } and the *edge value* is 2.

The *second rectangle corner* ("*cell2*") is cell H-8, in box 9, it's value is { 9 }.

The *third rectangle corner* ("*cell3*") is cell H-5, in box 8, it's value is { 5 }.

The details for Step (F) - (4), "*Check for the fourth corner*" are:

- *cell1* is in row C, and *cell3* is in column 5, so *cell4* is in row C, column 5; it's value is { 9 }.
- *cell4* is in box 2; the *edge value*, 2, is in box 2 two times.
- *cell4* satisfies H1 - H4 :

    ♦ H1 *cell4* does not have 2 as a candidate
    ♦ H2 *cell4*'s row segment and column segment have all of the candidates for 2.
    ♦ H3 *cell4*'s row segment has one cell with 2 as a candidate.
    ♦ H4 *cell4*'s column segment has one cell with 2 as a candidate.

- So the value 2 can be purged from cell C-8.

	Col 1	Col 2	Col 3	Col 4	Col 5	Col 6	Col 7	Col 8	Col 9
A	8	1 2 3 4	1 2 4 6	1 5 6	2 3	1 5	2 3 4	7	9
B	6 9	1 2 3 9	1 2 3 6	1 6	7	4	2 3	5	8
C	3 4	5	7	8	9	2 3	6	2 3 4	1
D	3 4	8	9	2 5	6	2 5	1	3 4	7
E	2	7	3 6	4	1	9	5 8	3 6 8	3 5
F	5 6	1 4	1 4 5 6	3	8	7	9	2 4 6	2 4
G	5 9	2 3	2 3	7 9	4	8	5 7	1	6
H	7	6	8	1 2	5	1 2 3	2 3 4	9	2 4
I	1	4 9	4 5	7 9	2 3	6	5 7 8	2 3 8	3 5

After purging cell C-8

A number of eliminations follow when cell C-8 is changed to { 3, 4 }, enough so that the puzzle can easily be solved.

- In row C, cell C-6 now has the only candidate for 2, so it can be changed to 2.
- Cell A-5 can be changed to 3.
- Cell I-5 can be changed to 2.
- Cell H-4 can be changed to 1.
- Cell B-4 can be changed to 6.
- Cell B-1 can be changed to 9.
- Cell A-4 can be changed to 5.
- Cell A-6 can be changed to 1.
- Cell D-4 can be changed to 2.
- Cell D-6 can be changed to 5.
- Note that column 8 now has only one candidate for 2 (cell I-5 is 2) - cell F-8, so F-8 can be changed to 2.

The remaining steps to solve the puzzle are straightforward.

Exocet Technique

The *"Junior Exocet" (JExocet) Technique* uses a complicated pattern involving:

- two Base Cells
- two Target Cells
- a Companion Cell for the first Target
- a Companion Cell for the second Target
- a Mirror Node consisting of two *near by(*)* cells for the first Target
- a Mirror Node consisting of two *near by(*)* cells for the second Target
- three sets of six "S Cells" that are outside of the base- and targets- boxes, as shown in the example patterns below.

There are two main patterns for JExocets, a three digit pattern and a four digit pattern. Both patterns may be either row-based or column-based. And a pattern may be either *diagonal* or *aligned*. Examples of the pattern layouts are shown below.

The candidate values in the Base Cells are termed "base candidates", or base candidate values. One such value is a "base digit". A three digit JExocet pattern has three "base digit" values, and a four digit pattern has four "base digit" values.

A candidate value that is not one of the base digits is termed a "non-base digit".

A "true" base digit is a base digit value in one of the Base Cells that agrees with the puzzle solution. It is unknown which base digit values are "true".

(*) The *near by* cells are in the same box; and are in the same row for a row-based pattern, or same column for a column-based pattern.

The pattern cell identifiers are:

- **B1, B2** identify the two Base Cells
- **T1, T2** identify Target one and Target two
- **C1, C2** identify the Companion Cells for T1 and T2
- **M1** identifies each cell in the T1 mirror node
- **M2** identifies each cell in the T2 mirror node
- **S** identifies the S Cells
- an unknown / don't care cell is shown as blank

To be a valid JExocet the following Pattern Requirements must be satisfied:

1. Each Base Cell must have 2, 3 or 4 digits ("base digits").
2. Together both Base Cells must contain 3 or 4 digits (base digits).
3. Each Target Cell must contain one or more base digits, and have two or more values.
4. Together both Target Cells must contain all of the base digits.
5. The Companion Cells don't contain any base digits.
6. Each Mirror Node must contain one or more base digits.

7. There must be at least two different base digits in { T1 and the Mirror Node for T2 }
8. There must be at least two different base digits in { T2 and the Mirror Node for T1 }
9. Considering the 18 S cells, each base digit must be a candidate value in no more than two of the columns for the S cells, or in no more than two of the rows for the S cells (this is termed "coverage").

S cell coverage requirement example for a row-based JExocet Pattern:

- The pattern is invalid if a base digit is in all three S cell columns, and in three or more of the six S cell rows.

It is important to note that for the Puzzle Solution, each Base Cell will contain only a single "true" base digit, correspondingly the rest of the base cell's row (for a row-based pattern) and the rest of the base cell's box won't contain the two "true" base digits (for a column-based pattern, the rest of the base cell's column won't contain the two "true" base digits).

For the Puzzle Solution the value of the T1 cell will be a single "true" base digit value; the value of the T2 cell will be different than T1 and will be a single "true" base digit value.

Row-based JExocet Patterns

The row-based *diagonal* JExocet pattern has the following layout considerations.

1. The two Base Cells are in the same row and the same box.
2. The two Target Cells are in different boxes and rows than the base cells; in rows that intersect the base-box.
3. Each Target Cell is in a different row and box.
4. C1 is in the same column as T1 and the same row as T2.
5. C2 is in the same column as T2 and the same row as T1.
6. The mirror node cells for T1 are in the same row and box as T2, in the two columns other than the T2 column.
7. The mirror node cells for T2 are in the same row and box as T1, in the two columns other than the T1 column.
8. The first group of six S cells are in rows that are outside of the base- box, and are in a column intersecting the base- box that is different than the columns for the base cells.
9. The second group of six S cells are in rows that are outside of the target-1 box, and are in the same column as the T1 cell.
10. The third group of six S cells are in rows that are outside of the target-2 box, and are in the same column as the T2 cell.

Purge Rules for Row-based JExocet Patterns

These Purge (elimination) rules are exemplified in the JExocet example puzzles. For column-based JExocet patterns the rules are stated in a separate section.

JExocet Purge Rule "E1"

Purge Rule E1 / Row, *"A base candidate that is restricted to one cover house is false in the base cell row-segment and in the Target cells."*

JExocet Purge Rule "E2"

Purge Rule E2, *"a base candidate that can't be true in at least one { Target and it's mirror node } is false."* Note that this rule should be re-considered if the other rules make changes.

JExocet Purge Rule "E3"

Purge Rule E3, *"any non-base candidate in a target is false".*

JExocet Purge Rule "E6"

Purge Rule E6, *"any base candidate that is not in a mirror node is false in the corresponding target".*

JExocet Purge Rule "E7"

Purge Rule E7, *"if one mirror cell can only contain non-base digits, the second mirror cell will be restricted to the base digit(s) in the opposite 'object cells' (target)."*

JExocet Purge Rule "E8"

Purge Rule E8 / Row, *"if a Mirror Node has only one non-base digit, it is true in the Mirror Node; so can be purged from the block and the row."*

JExocet Purge Rule "E9"

Purge Rule E9 / Row, *"if both cells of a Mirror Node have a non-base candidate that doesn't occur in the row for the other boxes, then any other non-base candidates are false in the mirror node."*

Example JExocet row-based, diagonal, pattern

	Col 1	Col 2	Col 3	Col 4	Col 5	Col 6	Col 7	Col 8	Col 9
Row A	B1	B2							
Row B				T1	M2	M2	C2		
Row C				C1			T2	M1	M1
Row D			S	S			S		
Row E			S	S			S		
Row F			S	S			S		
Row G			S	S			S		
Row H			S	S			S		
Row I			S	S			S		

The row-based *aligned* JExocet pattern has layout considerations 1, 2, 8, 9 and 10 the same as for the diagonal pattern (given above); and has these differences for layout considerations 3 through 7 above:

3. The two Target Cells are in the same row; in different boxes.
4. C1 is in the same column as T1 and in a different row than the Base Cells.
5. C2 is in the same column as T2 and is in the same row as C1.
6. The mirror node cells for T1 are in the same box as T2, in the same row as C2.
7. The mirror node cells for T2 are in the same box as T1, in the same row as C1.

Example JExocet row-based, aligned, pattern

	Col 1	Col 2	Col 3	Col 4	Col 5	Col 6	Col 7	Col 8	Col 9
Row A	B1	B2							
Row B				T1			T2		
Row C				C1	M2	M2	C2	M1	M1
Row D			S	S			S		
Row E			S	S			S		
Row F			S	S			S		
Row G			S	S			S		
Row H			S	S			S		
Row I			S	S			S		

Example Puzzle no. 1

This puzzle has a three valued, row-based, diagonal JExocet pattern. The base values are 1, 2 and 4. The Base Cells are Row A, Columns 1 and 2.

T1 is cell Row B, Column 4 and T2 is cell Row C, Column 7.

C1 is cell Row C, Column 4 and C2 is cell Row B, Column 7.

The Mirror node 1 cells are Row C, Columns 8 and 9.

The Mirror node 2 cells are Row B, Columns 5 and 6.

The S cells are all in Rows D - I, in columns 3, 4 and 7.

Example Puzzle no. 1 Overview

	Col 1	Col 2	Col 3	Col 4	Col 5	Col 6	Col 7	Col 8	Col 9
A	1 2 4	1 2	7	1 2 3 4 9	1 2 3 6 9	5	1 2 4 6 9	1 4 6 9	8
B	9	1 2 5 8	1 2 4 5 8	1 2 4 8	1 2 6 8	4 6 8	3	1 4 5 6 7	4 5 6 7
C	6	3	1 2 4 5 8	7	1 2 8 9	4 8 9	1 2 4 9	1 4 5 9	4 5 9
D			S	S			S		
E			S	S			S		
F			S	S			S		
G			S	S			S		
H			S	S			S		
I			S	S			S		

Example Puzzle no. 1 Complete

	Col 1	Col 2	Col 3	Col 4	Col 5	Col 6	Col 7	Col 8	Col 9
A	1 2 4	1 2	7	1 2 3 / 4 9	1 2 3 / 6 9	5	1 2 4 / 6 9	1 4 6 / 9	8
B	9	1 2 5 / 8	1 2 4 / 5 8	1 2 4 / 8	1 2 6 / 8	4 6 8	3	1 4 5 / 6 7	4 5 6 / 7
C	6	3	1 2 4 / 5 8	7	1 2 8 / 9	4 8 9	1 2 4 / 9	1 4 5 / 9	4 5 9
D	1 2 5 / 7	1 2 5 / 6 7 9	1 2 5 / 6	2 3 8 / 9	4	3 6 7 / 8 9	1 6 8 / 9	1 3 5 / 6 8 9	3 5 6 / 9
E	8	5 6 7 / 9	4 5 6	3 9	3 6 7 / 9	1	4 6 9	3 4 5 / 6 9	2
F	1 2 4	1 2 6 / 9	3	5	2 6 8 / 9	6 8 9	7	1 4 6 / 8 9	4 6 9
G	1 2 3 / 7	1 2 7 / 8	9	6	1 3 7 / 8	3 4 7 / 8	5	3 4 7 / 8	3 4 7
H	3 5 7	4	5 6 8	3 8 9	3 5 7 / 8 9	2	6 8 9	3 6 7 / 8 9	1
I	1 3 5 / 7	1 5 6 / 7 8	1 5 6 / 8	1 3 4 / 8 9	1 3 5 / 7 8 9	3 4 7 / 8 9	4 6 8 / 9	2	3 4 6 / 7 9

Checking the JExocet Pattern Requirements for Example 1

Checking the Pattern Requirements:

1. Each base cell has 2 or 3 base digits
2. Together both base cells contain all three base digits, { 1, 2, 4 }
3. T1 has base digits and has 4 values; and T2 has base digits and has 4 values
4. Together both target cells contain all three base digits, { 1, 2, 4 }
5. C1 and C2 don't have any base digits
6. Mirror node 1 has base digits, and mirror node 2 has base digits
7. { T1 and mirror node 2 } have 2 or more base digits
8. { T2 and mirror node 1 } have 2 or more base digits
9. S cell requirements:
   - base digit 1 is in Row D, Columns 3 and 7,
     and Row I, Columns 3 and 4, so is "covered" by two rows.

57

- base digit 2 is in Row D, Columns 3 and 4, so is "covered" by **one row**.
- base digit 4 is in Row E, Columns 3 and 7,
  and Row I, Column 7, so is "covered" by two rows.

JExocet Purging Considerations for Example 1

With the JExocet pattern verified, there is one consideration for purging candidate values. For the Example 1 puzzle, one of the JExocet Purge (elimination) Rules applies, which leads to four purges as explained below.

JExocet Purge Rule "E1"

Purge Rule E1 / Row, *"A base candidate that is restricted to one cover house is False in the base cell row-segment and in the Target cells."*

Base digit 2 in only one of the S cell rows (for the columns involved, columns 3, 4 and 7). So the value can be purged as follows:

- purge the base cell row segment (row A, columns 1 - 3) - set cell Row A, Column 1 to { 1, 4 }, and set cell Row A, Column 2 to { 1 }.
  (so cell Row A, Column 1 can be set to { 4 })
- purge Target 1 - set cell Row B, Column 4 to { 1, 4, 8 }.
- purge Target 2 - set cell Row C, Column 7 to { 1, 4, 9 }.

Example Puzzle no. 2-A

This puzzle has a four valued, row-based, diagonal JExocet pattern. The base values are 1, 2, 3 and 4. The Base Cells are Row G, Columns 8 and 9.

T1 is cell Row I, Column 2 and T2 is cell Row H, Column 6.

C1 is cell Row H, Column 2 and C2 is cell Row I, Column 6.

Mirror node 1 is cells Row H, Column 4 and Row H, Column 5.

Mirror node 2 is cells Row I, Column 1 and Row I, Column 3.

The S cells are all in Rows A - F, in columns 2, 6 and 7.

Example Puzzle no. 2-A Overview

	Col 1	Col 2	Col 3	Col 4	Col 5	Col 6	Col 7	Col 8	Col 9
A		S				S	S		
B		S				S	S		
C		S				S	S		
D		S				S	S		
E		S				S	S		
F		S				S	S		
G	2 3 4 5 7 9	1 2 3 4 9	1 2 3 7 9	1 3 5 8 9	1 2 4 5 8 9	1 2 3 5 9	6	1 2 3	1 2 3 4
H	2 3 4 9	8	1 2 3 9	1 3 6 9	1 2 4 6 9	1 2 3 9	1 2 3 4	5	7
I	2 3 4 5	1 2 3 4	6	1 3 5	1 2 4 5	7	1 2 3 4	8	9

Example Puzzle no. 2-A Complete

	Col 1	Col 2	Col 3	Col 4	Col 5	Col 6	Col 7	Col 8	Col 9
A	1	3 4 9	3 8 9	2	5 7 8 9	3 5 9	3 4 5	3 6 7	3 4 5 6
B	2 3 9	6	5	1 3 7 9	1 7 9	4	8	1 2 3 7	1 2 3
C	2 3 4 8	7	2 3 8	1 3 5 8	1 5 8	6	9	1 2 3	1 2 3 4 5
D	2 3 6 7 8	1 2 3	4	1 5 6 7	1 2 5 6 7	1 2 5	1 2 3 5	9	1 2 3 5 6 8
E	2 3 6 9	5	1 2 3 9	4	1 2 6 9	8	7	1 2 3 6	1 2 3 6
F	2 6 7 8 9	1 2 9	1 2 7 8 9	1 5 6 7 9	3	1 2 5 9	1 2 5	4	1 2 5 6 8
G	2 3 4 5 7 9	1 2 3 4 9	1 2 3 7 9	1 3 5 8 9	1 2 4 5 8 9	1 2 3 5 9	6	1 2 3	1 2 3 4
H	2 3 4 9	8	1 2 3 9	1 3 6 9	1 2 4 6 9	1 2 3 9	1 2 3 4	5	7
I	2 3 4 5	1 2 3 4	6	1 3 5	1 2 4 5	7	1 2 3 4	8	9

Verifying the JExocet Pattern for Example 2-A

Verifying the Pattern Requirements:

1. Each base cell has 3 or 4 base digits
2. Together both base cells contain all four base digits, { 1, 2, 3, 4 }
3. T1 has base digits and has 4 values; and T2 has base digits and has 4 values
4. Together both target cells contain all four base digits, { 1, 2, 3, 4 }
5. C1 and C2 don't have any base digits
6. Mirror node 1 has base digits, and mirror node 2 has base digits
7. { T1 and mirror node 2 } have 2 or more base digits
8. { T2 and mirror node 1 } have 2 or more base digits
9. S cell requirements:
   - base digit 1 is in Row D, Columns 2, 6 and 7,

60

and Row F, Columns 2, 6 and 7, so is "covered" by two rows.

- base digit 2 is in Row D, Columns 2, 6 and 7,
  and Row F, Columns 2, 6 and 7, so is covered by two rows.
- base digit 3 is in Row A, Columns 2, 6 and 7,
  and Row D, Columns 2 and 7, so is covered by two rows.
- base digit 4 is in Row A, Columns 2 and 7,
  and Row B, Column 6, so is covered by two rows.

JExocet Purging Considerations for Example 2-A

With the JExocet pattern verified, there are several considerations for purging candidate values. For the Example 2-A puzzle, four of the JExocet Purge (elimination) Rules apply, which lead to five purges as explained below.

JExocet Purge Rule "E3"

Purge Rule E3, *"any non-base candidate in a target is false"*.

T2 contains the value 9, which isn't a base candidate. So the value can be purged from T2 - set cell Row H, Column 6 to { 1, 2, 3 }.

JExocet Purge Rule "E6"

Purge Rule E6, *"any base candidate that is not in a mirror node is false in the corresponding target"*.

Mirror node 2 contains { 2, 3, 4, 5, 6 }, so the base candidate value 1 can be purged from T2 - set cell Row H, Column 6 to { 2, 3 } (this is the second purge for this cell).

JExocet Purge Rule "E7"

Purge Rule E7, *"if one mirror cell can only contain non-base digits, the second mirror cell will be restricted to the base digit(s) in the opposite 'object cells' (target)."*

Mirror cell Row I, Column 3 (for Mirror node 2) has the value { 6 } - only non-base digit(s). So mirror cell Row I, Column 1 (for Mirror node 2) (value { 2, 3, 4, 5 }) is restricted to the base digits in T2, which are { 1, 2, 3 } so 4 can be purged - set cell Row I, Column 1 to { 2, 3, 5 }.

JExocet Purge Rule "E9"

Purge Rule E9 / Row, *"if both cells of a Mirror Node have a non-base candidate that doesn't occur in the row for the other boxes, then any other non-base candidates are false in the mirror node."*

The cells for Mirror node 1, Row H Columns 4 and 5, both have 6, which is a non-base candidate, and 6 only occurs in Row H in these two cells. Mirror node 1 contains { 1, 2, 3, 4, 6, 9 }, so the non-base candidate value 9 can be removed from the mirror node. Set cell Row H, Column 4 to { 1, 3, 6 } and set cell Row H, Column 5 to { 1, 2, 4, 6 }.

Example Puzzle no. 2-B

This puzzle has a four valued, row-based, diagonal JExocet pattern. The base values are 1, 2, 3 and 4. The Base Cells are Row G, Columns 8 and 9.

T1 is cell Row I, Column 3 and T2 is cell Row H, Column 6.

C1 is cell Row H, Column 3 and C2 is cell Row I, Column 6.

Mirror node 1 is cells Row H, Columns 4 and 5.

Mirror node 2 is cells Row I, Columns 1 and 2.

The S cells are all in Rows A - F, in columns 3, 6 and 7.

Example Puzzle no. 2-B Complete

	Col 1	Col 2	Col 3	Col 4	Col 5	Col 6	Col 7	Col 8	Col 9
A	5 6 7 8	2	1 7 8	3	4 6 7 8 9	4 6 8	1 4 5 9	1 5 6 7 9	1 4 5 6
B	4	5 6 7 8	3 7 8	2 6 7 8 9	1	2 6 8	2 3 5 9	2 3 5 6 7 9	2 3 5 6
C	3 6 7	1 6 7	9	2 4 6 7	4 6 7	5	8	1 2 3 6 7	1 2 3 4 6
D	1	4 6 7 8 9	4 7 8	4 6 7 8	2	3 4 6 8	3 5 9	3 5 6 9	3 5 6 8
E	2 6 8	4 6 8	5	1 4 6 8	3 4 6 8	9	7	1 2 3 6	1 2 3 6 8
F	2 6 7 8 9	3	2 7 8	5	6 7 8	1 6 8	1 2 9	4	1 2 6 8
G	2 3 7 8 9	1 4 7 8 9	1 2 3 4 7 8	1 2 4 8 9	5	1 2 3 4 8	6	1 2 3	1 2 3 4
H	2 3 5 8 9	1 4 5 8 9	6	1 2 4 8 9	3 4 8 9	1 2 3 4 8	1 2 3 4 5	1 2 3 5	7
I	2 3 5	1 4 5	1 2 3 4	1 2 4 6	3 4 6	7	1 2 3 4 5	8	9

Verifying the JExocet Pattern for Example 2-B

Verifying the Pattern Requirements:

1. Each base cell has 3 or 4 base digits
2. Together both base cells contain all four base digits, { 1, 2, 3, 4 }
3. T1 has base digits and has 4 values; and T2 has base digits and has 5 values
4. Together both target cells contain all four base digits, { 1, 2, 3, 4 }
5. C1 and C2 don't have any base digits
6. Mirror node 1 has base digits, and mirror node 2 has base digits
7. { T1 and mirror node 2 } have 2 or more base digits
8. { T2 and mirror node 1 } have 2 or more base digits
9. S cell requirements:
   - base digit 1 is in Row A, Columns 3 and 7,
     and Row F, Columns 6 and 7, so is "covered" by two rows.
   - base digit 2 is in Row B, Columns 6 and 7,
     and Row F, Columns 3 and 7, so is covered by two rows.
   - base digit 3 is in Row B, Columns 3 and 7,
     and Row D, Columns 6 and 7, so is covered by two rows.
   - base digit 4 is in Row A, Columns 6 and 7,
     and Row D, Columns 3 and 6, so is covered by two rows.

JExocet Purging Considerations for Example 2-B

With the JExocet pattern verified there are two considerations for purging candidate values, for JExocet Purge (elimination) Rules **E3** and **E8**. This leads to four purges as described below.

JExocet Purge Rule "E3"

Purge Rule E3, *"any non-base candidate in a target is false"*.

T2 (cell Row H, Column 6) contains the value 8, which isn't a base candidate. So the value can be purged from T2.

Change cell H-6 from { 1, 2, 3, 4, 8 } to { 1, 2, 3, 4 }.

JExocet Purge Rule "E8"

Purge Rule E8 / Row, *"if a Mirror Node has only one non-base digit, it is true in the Mirror Node; so can be purged from the block and the row."*

Mirror node 2 contains { 1, 2, 3, 4, 5 }, only one non-base digit, 5. So :

- 5 can be purged from the "other" cells in it's box, box 7, i.e. cells G-1, G-2, G-3, H-1, H-2 and H-3.
- 5 can be purged from the row segments for Row I in boxes 8 and 9, i.e. for cells I-4 through I-9.

Change cell H-1 from { 2, 3, 5, 8, 9 } to { 2, 3, 8, 9 }. And **change cell H-2** from { 1, 4, 5, 8, 9 } to { 1, 4, 8, 9 }.

Change cell I-7 from { 1, 2, 3, 4, 5 } to { 1, 2, 3, 4 }.

Column-based JExocet Patterns

The column-based *diagonal* JExocet pattern has the following layout considerations.

1. The two Base Cells are in the same column and the same box.
2. The two Target Cells are in different boxes and columns than the base cells; in columns that intersect the base-box.
3. Each Target Cell is in a different column and box.
4. C1 is in the same row as T1 and the same column as T2.
5. C2 is in the same row as T2 and the same column as T1.
6. The mirror node cells for T1 are in the same column and box as T2, in the two rows other than the T2 row.
7. The mirror node cells for T2 are in the same column and box as T1, in the two rows other than the T1 row.
8. The first group of six S cells are in columns that are outside of the base- box, and are in a row intersecting the base- box that is different than the rows for the base cells.
9. The second group of six S cells are in columns that are outside of the target-1 box, and are in the same row as the T1 cell.
10. The third group of six S cells are in columns that are outside of the target-2 box, and are in the same row as the T2 cell.

Purge Rules for Column-based JExocet Patterns

These Purge (elimination) rules are exemplified in the JExocet example puzzles. The row-based JExocet pattern rules are stated in a separate section.

JExocet Purge Rule "E1"

Purge Rule E1 / Column, *"A base candidate that is restricted to one cover house is False in the base cell column-segment and in the Target cells."*

JExocet Purge Rule "E2"

Purge Rule E2, *"a base candidate that can't be true in at least one { Target and it's mirror node } is false."* Note that this rule should be re-considered if the other rules make changes.

JExocet Purge Rule "E3"

Purge Rule E3, *"any non-base candidate in a target is false"*.

JExocet Purge Rule "E6"

Purge Rule E6, *"any base candidate that is not in a mirror node is false in the corresponding target"*.

JExocet Purge Rule "E7"

Purge Rule E7, *"if one mirror cell can only contain non-base digits, the second mirror cell will be restricted to the base digit(s) in the opposite 'object cells' (target)."*

JExocet Purge Rule "E8"

Purge Rule E8 / Column, *"if a Mirror Node has only one non-base digit, it is true in the Mirror Node; so can be purged from the block and the column."*

JExocet Purge Rule "E9"

Purge Rule E9 / Column, *"if both cells of a Mirror Node have a non-base candidate that doesn't occur in the column for the other boxes, then any other non-base candidates are false in the mirror node."*

Example column-based, diagonal, Pattern for JExocet

	Col 1	Col 2	Col 3	Col 4	Col 5	Col 6	Col 7	Col 8	Col 9
Row A	M2								
Row B	T1	C1		S	S	S	S	S	S
Row C	M2								
Row D		M1							
Row E		M1							
Row F	C2	T2		S	S	S	S	S	S
Row G				S	S	S	S	S	S
Row H			B1						
Row I			B2						

65

The column-based *aligned* JExocet pattern has layout considerations 1, 8, 9 and 10 the same as for the diagonal pattern (given above); and has these differences for layout considerations 2 through 7 above:

2. The two Target Cells are in a different column than the base cells and the column intersects the base-box; and are in different boxes than the base cells.
3. The two Target Cells are in the same column, and in different boxes.
4. C1 is in the same row as T1 and in a different column than the Base Cells.
5. C2 is in the same row as T2 and is in the same column as C1.
6. The mirror node cells for T1 are in the same box as T2, in the same column as C2.
7. The mirror node cells for T2 are in the same box as T1, in the same column as C1.

Example column-based, aligned, Pattern for JExocet

	Col 1	Col 2	Col 3	Col 4	Col 5	Col 6	Col 7	Col 8	Col 9
Row A		M2							
Row B	T1	C1		S	S	S	S	S	S
Row C		M2							
Row D		M1							
Row E		M1							
Row F	T2	C2		S	S	S	S	S	S
Row G				S	S	S	S	S	S
Row H			B1						
Row I			B2						

Example puzzle no. 3

This puzzle has a four valued, column-based, diagonal JExocet pattern. The base values are 1, 2, 3 and 4.

The Base Cells are Row H, Column 3 and Row I, Column 3.

T1 is cell Row B, Column 1 and T2 is cell Row F, Column 2.

C1 is cell Row B, Column 2 and C2 is cell Row F, Column 1.

Mirror node 1 is cells Row D, Column 2 and Row E, Column 2.

Mirror node 2 is cells Row A, Column 1 and Row C, Column 1.

The S cells are in Rows B, F and G, in columns 4 - 9.

Example Puzzle no. 3 Overview

	Col 1	Col 2	Col 3	Col 4	Col 5	Col 6	Col 7	Col 8	Col 9
A	2 3 4 5	2 3 4 9	2 3 4 5 7 9						
B	1 2 3 4	8	1 2 3 4 9	S	S	S	S	S	S
C	6	1 2 3 9	1 2 3 7 9						
D	1 3 4 5	1 3 4 6 9	1 3 4 5 8 9						
E	1 2 4 5	1 2 4 6 9	1 2 4 5 8 9						
F	7	1 2 3 9	1 2 3 5 9	S	S	S	S	S	S
G	1 2 3 4	1 2 3 4	6	S	S	S	S	S	S
H	8	5	1 2 3						
I	9	7	2 3 4						

Example Puzzle no. 3 Complete

	Col 1	Col 2	Col 3	Col 4	Col 5	Col 6	Col 7	Col 8	Col 9
A	2 3 4 5	2 3 4 9	2 3 4 5 7 9	2 6 7 8 9	2 3 6 9	2 3 6 7 8 9	2 3 4 8	2 3 9	1
B	1 2 3 4	8	1 2 3 4 9	1 2 9	5	1 2 3 9	7	6	3 4 9
C	6	1 2 3 9	1 2 3 7 9	1 2 7 8 9	1 2 3 9	4	5	2 3 9	3 8 9
D	1 3 4 5	1 3 4 6 9	1 3 4 5 8 9	1 5 6 7 9	1 4 6 9	1 5 6 7 9	1 3 8	3 5 7 9	2
E	1 2 4 5	1 2 4 6 9	1 2 4 5 8 9	3	1 2 4 6 9	1 2 5 6 7 9	1 8	5 7 9	7 8 9
F	7	1 2 3 9	1 2 3 5 9	1 2 5 9	8	1 2 5 9	6	4	3 9
G	1 2 3 4	1 2 3 4	6	1 2 5	7	1 2 3 5	9	8	3 4 5
H	8	5	**1 2 3**	4	1 2 3 6 9	1 2 3 6 9	2 3	2 3 7	3 6 7
I	9	7	**2 3 4**	2 5 6 8	2 3 6	2 3 5 6 8	2 3 4	1	3 4 5 6

Verifying the JExocet Pattern for example 3

Verifying the Pattern Requirements:

1. Each base cell has three base digits
2. Together both base cells contain all four base digits, { 1, 2, 3, 4 }
3. T1 has base digits and has 4 values; and T2 has base digits and has 4 values
4. Together both target cells contain all four base digits, { 1, 2, 3, 4 }
5. C1 and C2 don't have any base digits
6. Mirror node 1 has base digits, and mirror node 2 has base digits
7. { T1 and mirror node 2 } have 2 or more base digits
8. { T2 and mirror node 1 } have 2 or more base digits
9. S cell requirements:
    - base digit 1 is in Row B, Columns 4 and 6, and Row F, Columns 4 and 6,

and Row G, Columns 4 and 6, so is "covered" by two columns.

- base digit 2 is in Row B, Columns 4 and 6, and Row F, Columns 4 and 6, and Row G, Columns 4 and 6, so is covered by two columns.
- base digit 3 is in Row B, Columns 6 and 9, and Row F, Column 9, and Row G, Columns 6 and 9, so is covered by two columns.
- base digit 4 is in Row B, Column 9, and Row F, Column 8, and Row G, Column 9, so is covered by two columns.

JExocet Purging Considerations for Example 3

With the JExocet pattern verified, there are several considerations for purging candidate values. For the Example 3 puzzle, three of the JExocet Purge (elimination) Rules apply, which lead to three purges as explained below.

JExocet Purge Rule "E3"

Purge Rule E3, *"any non-base candidate in a target is false"*.

T2 contains the value 9, which isn't a base candidate. So the value can be purged from T2 - set cell Row F, Column 2 to { 1, 2, 3 }.

JExocet Purge Rule "E6"

Purge Rule E6, *"any base candidate that is not in a mirror node is false in the corresponding target"*.

Mirror node 2 contains { 2, 3, 4, 5, 6 }, so the base candidate value 1 can be purged from T2 - set cell Row F, Column 2 to { 2, 3 } (this is the second purge for this cell).

JExocet Purge Rule "E7"

Purge Rule E7, *"if one mirror cell can only contain non-base digits, the second mirror cell will be restricted to the base digit(s) in the opposite 'object cells' (target)."*

Mirror cell Row C, Column 1 (for Mirror node 2) has the value { 6 } - only non-base digit(s). So mirror cell Row A, Column 1 (for Mirror node 2) (value { 2, 3, 4, 5 }) is restricted to the base digits in T2, which are { 1, 2, 3 } so 4 can be purged - set cell Row A, Column 1 to { 2, 3, 5 }.

Example puzzle no. 4

This puzzle has a four valued, column-based, diagonal JExocet pattern. The base values are 1, 2, 3 and 4.

The Base Cells are Row A, Column 7 and Row B, Column 7.

T1 is cell Row D, Column 8 and T2 is cell Row H, Column 9.

C1 is cell Row D, Column 9 and C2 is cell Row H, Column 8.

Mirror node 1 is cells Row G, Column 9 and Row I, Column 9.

Mirror node 2 is cells Row E, Column 8 and Row F, Column 8.

The S cells are in Rows C, D and H, in columns 1 - 6.

Example Puzzle no. 4 Overview

	Col 1	Col 2	Col 3	Col 4	Col 5	Col 6	Col 7	Col 8	Col 9
A							2 3 4	7	9
B							1 2 3	5	8
C	S	S	S	S	S	S	6	1 2 3 4	1 2 3 4
D	S	S	S	S	S	S	1 2 3 4 5	2 3 4	7
E							1 3 4 5 8	3 4 6 8	1 3 4 5
F							9	2 4 6 8	1 2 4 5
G							1 2 3 5 7 8	1 2 3 8	6
H	S	S	S	S	S	S	1 2 3 4 7	9	1 2 3 4
I							2 3 4 5 7 8	2 3 4 8	2 3 4 5

Example Puzzle no. 4 Complete

	Col 1	Col 2	Col 3	Col 4	Col 5	Col 6	Col 7	Col 8	Col 9
A	4 6 8	1 2 3 4	1 2 3 4 6	1 2 5 6 8	1 2 3	1 2 3 5 6 8	**2 3 4**	7	9
B	3 6 9	1 2 3 9	1 2 3 6	1 2 6 7	1 2 3 7	4	**1 2 3**	5	8
C	3 4 8	5	7	2 8	9	1 2 3 8	6	1 2 3 4	1 2 3 4
D	3 4 5	8	9	1 2 4 5	6	1 2 5	1 2 3 4 5	2 3 4	7
E	2	7	1 3 4 5 6	1 4 5 8	1 8	9	1 3 4 5 8	3 4 6 8	1 3 4 5
F	4 5 6	1 4	1 4 5 6	3	1 2 7 8	1 2 5 7	9	2 4 6 8	1 2 4 5
G	3 5 7 9	2 3 9	2 3 5	1 2 7 8 9	4	1 2 3 7 8	1 2 3 5 7 8	1 2 3 8	6
H	3 4 7	6	8	1 2 7	5	1 2 3 7	1 2 3 4 7	9	1 2 3 4
I	1	2 3 4 9	2 3 4 5	2 6 7 8 9	2 3 7 8	2 3 6 7 8	2 3 4 5 7 8	2 3 4 8	2 3 4 5

Verifying the JExocet Pattern for example 4

Verifying the Pattern Requirements:

1. Each base cell has three base digits
2. Together both base cells contain all four base digits, { 1, 2, 3, 4 }
3. T1 has base digits and has 3 values; and T2 has base digits and has 4 values
4. Together both target cells contain all four base digits, { 1, 2, 3, 4 }
5. C1 and C2 don't have any base digits
6. Mirror node 1 has base digits, and mirror node 2 has base digits
7. { T1 and mirror node 2 } have 2 or more base digits
8. { T2 and mirror node 1 } have 2 or more base digits
9. S cell requirements:
   - base digit 1 is in Row C, Column 6, and Row D, Columns 4 and 6,

71

and Row H, Columns 4 and 6, so is "covered" by two columns.

- base digit 2 is in Row C, Columns 4 and 6, and Row D, Columns 4 and 6, and Row H, Columns 4 and 6, so is covered by two columns.
- base digit 3 is in Row C, Columns 1 and 6, and Row D, Column 1, and Row H, Columns 1 and 6, so is covered by two columns.
- base digit 4 is in Row C, Column 1, and Row D, Columns 1 and 4, and Row H, Column 1, so is covered by two columns.

JExocet Purging Considerations for Example 4

With the JExocet pattern verified, there are two considerations for purging candidate values. For the Example 4 puzzle, two of the JExocet Purge (elimination) Rules apply, which lead to two purges as explained below.

JExocet Purge Rule "E6"

Purge Rule E6, *"any base candidate that is not in a mirror node is false in the corresponding target"*.

Mirror node 2 contains { 2, 3, 4, 6, 8 }, so the base candidate value 1 can be purged from T2 - set cell Row H, Column 9 to { 2, 3, 4 }.

JExocet Purge Rule "E2"

Purge Rule E2, *"a base candidate that can't be true in at least one { Target and it's mirror node } is false."* (this rule should be re-considered if the other rules make changes)

{ T1 and mirror node 1 } contain { 2, 3, 4, 6, 8 } - base candidate value 1 isn't included. And { T2 and mirror node 2 } contain { 2, 3, 4, 5, 6 } - base candidate value 1 isn't included. So the base candidate value 1 can be purged from B2 - set cell Row B, Column 7 to { 2, 3 }.

Appendix A BigFish Techniques

These techniques don't involve chaining. They consider a single candidate value and look for a pattern across sets of 4, 9 or 16 cells. If a pattern match is found then the candidate value can be purged from multiple cells as described below.

The techniques are named BigFish-2, BigFish-3 and BigFish-4 according to the number of cells in a row/column. The strategy may be known as *X-wing* for 2 cells in a row/column, or *Swordfish* for 3 cells in a row/column. The patterns are:

BigFish-2, <u>4 cells</u>

> two rows having the candidate value in the same two columns only,
> or two columns having the candidate value in the same two rows only.

BigFish-3, <u>9 cells</u>

> three rows having the candidate value in the same three columns only,
> or three columns having the candidate value in the same three rows only.

BigFish-4, <u>16 cells</u>

> four rows having the candidate value in the same four columns only,
> or four columns having the candidate value in the same four rows only.

For Mega Sudoku 16 x 16 puzzles an additional BigFish technique may be used. BigFish-5 for five rows or five columns corresponds directly the the other BigFish techniques.

BigFish-2 for Rows

This technique is performed for rows. It considers a single candidate value. The technique looks for a "first row" that has the candidate value in only two columns; and then a "second row" that has the candidate value in the same two columns only. The cells can have additional values.

Example: for some row the value 5 is only in columns "1" and "2", and another row also has the value 5 in columns "1" and "2" only.

If the pattern is matched the value can be removed from the other rows for the two columns involved.

BigFish-2 for Columns

This technique is performed for columns. It directly corresponds to BigFish-2 for Rows. The technique considers a single candidate value and looks for a "first column" that has the candidate value in only two rows; and then a "second column" that has the candidate value in the same two rows only. The cells can have additional values.

If the pattern is matched the value can be removed from the other columns for the two rows involved.

Example for BigFish-2 for Columns

An example is described for BigFish-2 for columns, using the partly solved example puzzle below. The example is for candidate value 8, and involves Columns 1 and 9, and Rows A and F. The cells that form the pattern are A-1, F-1, A-9 and F-9.

Candidate value 8 is in column 1 only in rows A and F. And Candidate value 8 is in column 9 only in rows A and F. This matches the BigFish-2 column pattern.

Candidate value **8 can be removed from cells A-8, F-3 and F-7**.

	Col 1	Col 2	Col 3	Col 4	Col 5	Col 6	Col 7	Col 8	Col 9
A	3 4 6 8	1 4 6 7	5	1 7 9	3 6 7 9	1 3 7 9	2	3 4 8 9	1 4 8 9
B	3 6	2	1 6	8	3 6 9	4	5	7	1 9
C	9	1 4 7	1 4 8	1 2 7	5	1 2 3 7	1 3 4 8	3 4 8	6
D	4 6	9	2 4 6 7	3	1	8	4 7	5	2 4 7
E	1	5	7 8	2 7 9	4	2 7 9	7 8 9	6	3
F	4 8	3	2 4 7 8	6	7 9	5	4 7 8 9	1	2 4 7 8 9
G	2	1 4	9	5	8	1 3 7	6	3 4	1 4 7
H	7	1 4 6	1 3 4 6	1 9	2	1 3 9	1 3 4 8 9	3 4 8 9	5
I	5	8	1 3	4	3 7 9	6	1 3 7 9	2	1 7 9

BigFish-3 for Rows

This technique extends *BigFish-2 for Rows* to three rows. It considers a single candidate value and looks for a pattern where each of three rows has the candidate value in two or three columns and all of the columns are the same. The pattern will have up to nine cells. There are two pattern variations:

- Pattern A (nine cells) :
    - A "first row" has the candidate value in three columns only
    - A "second row" has the candidate value in three columns only

- A "third row" has the candidate value in three columns only
- All of the columns are the same.
- The cells can have additional values.
- Pattern B (six - eight cells) :
  - A "first row" has the candidate value in only two or three columns
  - A "second row" has the candidate value in only two or three columns
  - A "third row" has the candidate value in only two or three columns
  - There are only three columns involved.
  - The cells can have additional values.

If the pattern is matched the value can be removed from the other rows for the columns involved.

Example for BigFish-3 for Rows

An example is described, using the partly solved example puzzle below.

This example is for Pattern B, with candidate value 9, and involves rows B, F and I, and columns 5, 7 and 9. The cells that form the pattern are B-5 and B-9; F-5, F-7 and F-9; I-5, I-7 and I-9.

Candidate value 9 is in Row B only in columns 5 and 9.

Candidate value 9 is in Row F only in columns 5, 7 and 9.

Candidate value 9 is in Row I only in columns 5, 7 and 9. This completes a pattern match for BigFish-3 for rows.

Candidate value **9 can be removed from cells A-5, E-7, H-7 and A-9**.

	Col 1	Col 2	Col 3	Col 4	Col 5	Col 6	Col 7	Col 8	Col 9
A	3 4 6 8	1 4 6 7	5	1 7 9	3 6 7 9	1 3 7 9	2	3 4 8 9	1 4 8 9
B	3 6	2	1 6	8	3 6 9	4	5	7	1 9
C	9	1 4 7	1 4 8	1 2 7	5	1 2 3 7	1 3 4 8	3 4 8	6
D	4 6	9	2 4 6 7	3	1	8	4 7	5	2 4 7
E	1	5	7 8	2 7 9	4	2 7 9	7 8 9	6	3
F	4 8	3	2 4 7 8	6	7 9	5	4 7 8 9	1	2 4 7 8 9
G	2	1 4	9	5	8	1 3 7	6	3 4	1 4 7
H	7	1 4 6	1 3 4 6	1 9	2	1 3 9	1 3 4 8 9	3 4 8 9	5
I	5	8	1 3	4	3 7 9	6	1 3 7 9	2	1 7 9

BigFish-3 for Columns

This technique extends *BigFish-2 for Columns* to three columns. It considers a single candidate value and looks for a pattern where each of three columns has the candidate value in two or three rows and all of the rows are the same. The pattern will have up to nine cells. There are two pattern variations:

- Pattern A (nine cells) :
  - A "first column" has the candidate value in three rows only
  - A "second column" has the candidate value in three rows only
  - A "third column" has the candidate value in three rows only
  - All of the rows are the same.
  - The cells can have additional values.
- Pattern B (six - eight cells) :
  - A "first column" has the candidate value in only two or three rows
  - A "second column" has the candidate value in only two or three rows
  - A "third column" has the candidate value in only two or three rows
  - There are only three rows involved.
  - The cells can have additional values.

If the pattern is matched the value can be removed from the other columns for the rows involved.

BigFish-4 for Rows

This technique extends *BigFish-3 for Rows* to four rows. It considers a single candidate value and looks for a pattern where each of four rows has the candidate value in two, three or four columns and all of the columns are the same. The pattern will have up to 16 cells. There are two pattern variations:

- Pattern A (16 cells) :
  - A "first row" has the candidate value in four columns only
  - A "second row" has the candidate value in four columns only
  - A "third row" has the candidate value in four columns only
  - A "fourth row" has the candidate value in four columns only
  - All of the columns are the same.
  - The cells can have additional values.
- Pattern B (eight - fifteen cells) :
  - A "first row" has the candidate value in only two - four columns
  - A "second row" has the candidate value in only two - four columns
  - A "third row" has the candidate value in only two - four columns
  - A "fourth row" has the candidate value in only two - four columns
  - There are only four columns involved.
  - The cells can have additional values.

If the pattern is matched the value can be removed from the other rows for the columns involved.

BigFish-4 for Columns

This technique extends *BigFish-3 for Columns* to four columns. It considers a single candidate value and looks for a pattern where each of four columns has the candidate value in two, three or four rows and all of the rows are the same. The pattern will have up to 16 cells. There are two pattern variations:

- Pattern A (16 cells) :
    - A "first column" has the candidate value in four rows only
    - A "second column" has the candidate value in four rows only
    - A "third column" has the candidate value in four rows only
    - A "fourth column" has the candidate value in four rows only
    - All of the rows are the same.
    - The cells can have additional values.
- Pattern B (eight - fifteen cells) :
    - A "first column" has the candidate value in only two - four rows
    - A "second column" has the candidate value in only two - four rows
    - A "third column" has the candidate value in only two - four rows
    - A "fourth column" has the candidate value in only two - four rows
    - There are only four rows involved.
    - The cells can have additional values.

If the pattern is matched the value can be removed from the other columns for the rows involved.

Example for BigFish-4 for Columns

An example is described, using the partly solved example puzzle below.

This example is for Pattern B, with candidate value 4, and involves rows A, E, F and I, and columns 3, 5, 7 and 8. The cells that form the pattern are A-3 and A-7;   E-5, E-7 and E-8; F-5 and F-7;   I-3 and I-8.

Candidate value 4 is in Row A only in columns 3 and 7.

Candidate value 4 is in Row E only in columns 5, 7 and 8.

Candidate value 4 is in Row F only in columns 5 and 7.

Candidate value 4 is in Row I only in columns 3 and 8. This completes a pattern match for BigFish-4 for columns.

Candidate value **4 can be removed from cells E-9 and F-9**.

	Col 1	Col 2	Col 3	Col 4	Col 5	Col 6	Col 7	Col 8	Col 9
A	6	1 2 3 5	1 2 3 4 5	1 2 3 5	1 2 3	8	1 2 3 4	7	9
B	3 7	1 2 3 7	1 2 3	9	6	4	1 2 3	5	8
C	3 4 5	8	9	1 2 3 5	7	1 2 5	6	1 2 3	1 2 3 4
D	3 5 9	4	6	1 2 5	8	1 2 5 9	1 2 3 5 9	2 3	7
E	5 7 8 9	1 5 7 9	1 5 8	6	1 2 4 9	3	1 2 4 5 8 9	1 2 4 9	1 2 4 5
F	2	1 3 5 9	1 3 5 8	7	1 4 9	1 5 9	1 3 4 5 8 9	6	1 3 4 5
G	3 5 8 9	2 3 5 9	2 3 5 8	4	1 2 3 9	7	1 2 3 5 9	1 2 3 9	6
H	3 4 9	6	7	1 2 3	5	1 2 9	1 2 3 9	8	1 2 4
I	1	2 3 5 9	2 3 4 5	8	2 3 9	6	7	2 3 4 9	2 3 5

Appendix B Two Segments Techniques

The techniques *Two Segments for Rows* and *Two Segments for Columns* are for 16 x 16 Sudoku puzzles only. They look for a pattern for a single candidate value, Chaining is not involved.

The related basic techniques named *One Segment for Rows* and *One Segment for Columns* are described in the Section *Background Techniques* - the *Two Segments* techniques are similar, but more complicated. The *One Segment* techniques are applicable to both 9 x 9 and 16 x 16 Sudoku puzzles. They look for a pattern for a single candidate value, chaining is not involved.

Two Segments for Rows

This technique is performed for rows, it considers a single candidate value. The technique looks for a pattern across a horizontal group of four boxes for the same rows, e.g. boxes 1 - 4 for rows A, B, C and D (may be termed rows 1, 2, 3 and 4).

To determine a pattern match:
- Look for a first box that has the candidate value in only two row segments.
- Look for a second box that has the candidate in only the two corresponding row segments.

If the pattern is matched the value can be removed from the corresponding row segments for the two other boxes.

For the similar technique Two Segments for Columns, a complete example is shown below.

Two Segments for Columns

This technique is performed for columns, it considers a single candidate value. The technique looks for a pattern across a vertical group of four boxes for the same columns, e.g. boxes 4, 8, 12 and 16 for columns 13, 14, 15 and 16.

To determine a pattern match:
- Look for a first box that has the candidate value in only two column segments.
- Look for a second box that has the candidate in only the two corresponding column segments.

If the pattern is matched the value can be removed from the corresponding column segments for the two other boxes.

Two Segments for Columns example

An example puzzle is shown below. The candidate value 8 is in box 4 only in columns 14 and 15; and 8 is in box 8 only in those two columns. So 8 can be purged for these cells (the cell locations are shown as "row-column", e.g. 9-14 for row 9 column 14):
- box 12 cells 9-14, 10-14, 11-14 and 12-14
- box 12 cells 9-15, 10-15, 11-15 and 12-15

- box 16 cells 13-14, 14-14, 15-14 and 16-14
- box 16 cells 13-15, 14-15, 15-15 and 16-15

Cell 10-15 in box 12 can be changed from { 8, 10, 14 } to { 10, 14 }.

As this leaves row 10 with only one cell having the candidate value 8, **cell 10-6 can be set to 8 now**. Consequently, **8 can be purged for cell 12-6**.

The column segments that form the pattern are shown highlighted. The cell values for the boxes of interest, 4, 8, 12 and 16 are shown in full. For the other boxes singleton (known) cell values are shown; an '&' character denotes a multi-valued, unknown cell that does not have 8 as a candidate; and '8&' indicates a multi-valued, unknown cell that has 8 as a candidate.

C 1	C 2	C 3	C 4	C 5	C 6	C 7	C 8	C 9	C 10	C 11	C 12	C 13	C 14	C 15	C 16
7	&	13	14	&	&	8	&	&	15	&	16	5	2 11	3 9	4
8	&	&	6	&	4	&	5	7	&	13	10	16	1	3 9	14
&	&	4	3	1	&	16	7	&	5	&	&	12	8 10	8 10	13
10	&	16	5	13	&	14	&	&	4	&	8	7	2 11	6	15
16	5	8&	8&	&	6	12	&	&	&	&	&	1 3 14	4 15	13	7
2	&	7	10	&	1	13	16	5	8&	8&	9	3 14	6	11 14	12
14	&	9	12	8	7	2	15	6	13	&	&	1 3 10	4 10	5	16
1	4	6	13	14	5	10	3	12	7	16	&	2	8 15	8 11	9
6	10	14	&	12	2	&	1	8	11	7	13	15	5	16	3
13	16	5	2	7	8&	&	&	&	&	&	&	11	9	8 10 14	1
&	8	12	&	16	&	11	13	&	1	&	5	4 10 14	7	2	6
&	7	&	&	5	8&	15	14	&	16	&	&	4 8 10	13	12	8 10
9	&	8&	8&	10	&	1	12	4	6	5	7	13	16	15	2 8
12	6	10	8&	2	&	7	4	13	8&	8&	&	8 9	14	1	5
4	&	8&	8&	&	13	5	8&	&	8&	10	12	6	3	7	11
5	13	15	7	&	&	&	8&	&	8&	&	&	8 9 10	12	4	2 8 10

Made in the USA
Monee, IL
01 August 2021